W.O. MITCHELL COUNTRY

M&S

[A DOUGLAS GIBSON BOOK]

W.O. MITCHELL COUNTRY

Portrayed by

Courtney Milne

Text by W.O. Mitchell · *Selected by Orm and Barbara Mitchell*

Canadian Cataloguing in Publication Data

Milne, Courtney, 1943-
    W.O. Mitchell country

ISBN 0-7710-6106-4

I. Landscape photography – Alberta. 2. Landscape photography –
Saskatchewan. 3. Alberta – Pictorial works. 4. Saskatchewan – Pictorial
works. 5. Milne, Courtney, 1943-   . I. Mitchell, W. O. (William Ormond),
1914-1998. II. Mitchell, Ormond. III. Mitchell, Barbara. IV. Title.

FC3662.M54 1999   779'.367123'092   C99-931225-1
F1076.8.M54 1999

We acknowledge the financial support of the Government of Canada through the Book Publishing Industry Development Program for our publishing activities. We further acknowledge the support of the Canada Council for the Arts and the Ontario Arts Council for our publishing program.

Canada

Book design by Kong Njo

Title-page image: *Stubble field, sunset light, near Eston, SK, 1981*

Printed and bound in Spain
D.L. TO: 1442-1999

A Douglas Gibson Book

McClelland & Stewart Inc.
The Canadian Publishers
481 University Avenue
Toronto, Ontario
M5G 2E9

1 2 3 4 5   03 02 01 00 99

For W.O., who invites us to hear the poetry of earth and sky

Outdoor mural by J.M. Compton, High River, AB, photographed 1998

Canola field near Humboldt, SK, 1998

CONTENTS

INTRODUCTION:

"The Poetry of Earth & Sky" 1

"An' There Was Heaven An' Earth" 3

Prairie 27

Foothills & Mountains 111

by Orm & Barbara Mitchell

Inscapes 187

by Courtney Milne

THE MAKING OF THE BOOK 228

ACKNOWLEDGEMENTS 231

Granaries and stubble field, near Marengo, SK, 1998

INTRODUCTION

"The Poetry of Earth & Sky"

"It's important for you to be able to hear 'the poetry of earth'." This was W.O. Mitchell's response to a young Vancouver high-school student who had written him in 1967 saying that *Who Has Seen the Wind* had made her cry. "I don't think it has changed my whole idea of life, but something has changed," she said. "I'm going to make sure if I have a family, I'll raise them all out on the prairies." W.O. assured her that "the poetry of earth" is not "one kind of poetry" but many: "It will sing to you and make you want to cry on the sea shore – in the mountains – the foothills – lake country. The important thing is to be able to hear that poetry, and from your letter I am sure you can. Don't ever forget how."

W.O. never forgot how, and he connected with "the poetry of earth and sky" in a number of places, but in particular on the Saskatchewan prairie and in the Alberta foothills and mountains.

When we were introduced to Courtney Milne's images through his earlier books, *Prairie Light*, *Prairie Dreams*, and *Prairie Skies*, we found this same "connectedness" with landscape and the same passion for capturing and celebrating the melodramatic skin of prairie landscape that is so characteristic of W.O.'s work. We knew that he was precisely the kind of creative partner that W.O. would have wanted for a book such as this, a landscape photographer who would play with his words, who would go beyond the literal and the ordinary. Shot through the filter of W.O.'s prose, Courtney's images of W.O. Mitchell country have a striking particularity and variety which give this book its distinctive character.

Orm and Barbara Mitchell
Peterborough, January 1999

Sunlight streaming through cloud, Saskatoon, SK, 1989

"An' There Was Heaven An' Earth"

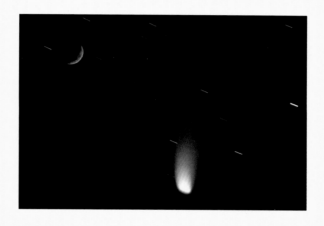

I M A G I N I N G   P L A C E

Throughout his life W.O. was engaged in a reciprocal relationship with place. Even as he was stained by his landscapes, he re-created them and gave these places rich inner meaning and significance for his readers. Over the years students who have never seen prairie but who have read *Who Has Seen the Wind* have told us, "I now *know* what prairie is like." While Saskatchewan prairie and Alberta foothills both put their stamps on W.O. — "signed" him — he in turn through his writing put his unique stamp on them — "signed" them.

W.O. believed that "all art is one and indivisible." Whatever medium the creative sensibility uses, it seeks to explore those universal "skeleton" questions at the centre of our existence. Just as W.O. argued that there were deeper meanings below the surface of his prairie descriptions, that they were not "photographic realism," Courtney Milne's photographs take the viewer far beyond a documentary replication of prairie and foothills. His celluloid is not simply a passive *tabula rasa* that reflects, casually and randomly,

Inset: Double exposure of moon with time exposure of Hale Bopp comet and stars, Grandora, SK, 1997

good-looking images. His images travel into prairie and foothills much more deeply than the everyday eye most of us bring to these places. Courtney's eye searches for and communicates what is symbolic and evocative about a "place." He uses camera angle and movement, lens, light, filter, and multiple exposure to shape and give aesthetic and spiritual significance to places and to convey their emotional and psychological impact on human consciousness.

In one of the stories from *Jake and the Kid*, the Kid uses a striking image to describe young wheat: "There isn't any green like young wheat green stretching out spang to the horizon, bright green like to yell at a person." Bright green that yells. The image blends the senses of sight and sound. Miss Henchbaw, the Kid's teacher, would have pointed out that he was using the poetic technique of "synaesthesia," Greek for "perceiving together." This book of words and images creates, we think successfully, the same effect — a cross-fertilizing of W.O.'s words and Courtney's images to convey both the outer and inner dimensions of W.O.'s country.

Courtney's images, while making their own unique statements about prairie and foothills landscapes, beautifully complement W.O.'s word pictures of these same land-scapes. Sometimes the relationship between word and image is literal. But often we have tried for less tangible connections, for a complementary meeting of Courtney's and W.O.'s "inscapes" — such as Courtney's use of camera tilt and movement to capture W.O.'s analo-gy of the prairie's "superlative sun" and "grass sea" to Homer's Aegean Sea; or the images which suggest his characters' "self-erasure" and melding with river, rock, cloud, "magic land flow"; or the opening series of abstract images complementing Saint Sammy's version of the creation of the world.

And now it is time to get personal. Both of us — Orm, W.O.'s elder son, and Barbara, who plays the role of Merna in the household — have been deeply immersed in W.O.'s life and work as we prepare a two-volume biography. Creating this book with Courtney had a poignant dimension for us, but it has been a rewarding and fascinating experience. Seeing W.O.'s country through the eyes of a photographer who captures the minute world at his feet, the bare essentials of the landscape, and the dramatic cloudscapes has re-energized W.O.'s prose for us. We were inspired to reread his descriptions closely and see in our mind's eye the particularities of his places. Revisiting Weyburn prairie,

High River, and the Eden Valley with Courtney made us see these places with new eyes. We were delighted in particular to show Courtney the foothills country in which we (both High River kids) were raised and which formed our identity contracts with ourselves for the rest of our lives. Although we have lived in Ontario's Kawartha Lakes country since 1971, we have been drawn back at least twice a year to the Alberta foothills. And while Baker Creek, a tributary to the Highwood a few miles west of High River, is now only a meandering series of grassed over hollows and its swimming holes and trout pools are now only echoes in our memories, the Highwood is the same glacial river cutting through shale banks and canyons. The saskatoon bushes along the river road, although much higher and denser than we remember, still yield berries for the best-tasting pies in the world. At Cat Creek camp, as Courtney and Sherrill absorbed the Highwood and its Rockies for the first time, a grey hackled dry fly drew the same silver-flash strikes we had thrilled to forty years and more ago.

We have over the years regularly revisited our foothills country, but this trip back was particularly special. We reconnected with our childhood places around High River and in the Eden Valley — not only last August as we showed Courtney where we had hunted ducks and geese at Frank Lake, or where we had fished the Highwood in Eden Valley and the canyon — but also sitting in the dark of our basement in Peterborough last December, and again later in January in a dark windowless conference room at the Delta Bessborough Hotel in Saskatoon, as we watched image after image of our place flash on the screen. Courtney's images, like W.O.'s descriptions, invite us to see and feel familiar places afresh, and surprise us by magically revealing new landscapes under old. Plato's parable of the chained prisoners in a cave comes to mind — but unlike his prisoners who are mesmerized by flickering third-hand imitations of the Real, we sense we are released into a deeper seeing by these magic-lantern images on the screen.

With his stomach delightfully anxious, Brian stared at Saint Sammy. The old man walked a step away, then wheeled with his long arm up. . . .

"What's Heaven like?" asked Ike. On the way out he had told Brian and Fat that Saint Sammy really got going when he talked about Heaven and how God made the world. . . .

"What's Heaven like?" asked Ike. "What's it like, Sammy?"

In a monotone, with the sing-songing stress of a child's Christmas recitation, Saint Sammy began:

"To start with He give a flip to the fly-wheel a thought, an' there was Heaven an' earth an' Him plumb in the middle. She had no shape ner nothin' on her. 'Let there be light,' He seth, an' there was some. 'Suits me fine,' He seth, 'an' I'm a-gonna call her night, an' I'm a-gonna call her day.' He took an' He gathered all the water together so the dry land stuck up; 'that there is dry earth,' He seth. 'Grass,' He seth, 'let her come.' An' she come. She jumped up green. He hung up the moon; he stuck up the sun; he pricked out the stars. He rigged out spring an' fall an' winter an' He done it. He made Him some fishes to use the sea fer swimmin' in — some fowls fer to use the air fer flyin' in."

WHO HAS SEEN THE WIND

Sunset light on cloud front, Grandora, SK, 1998

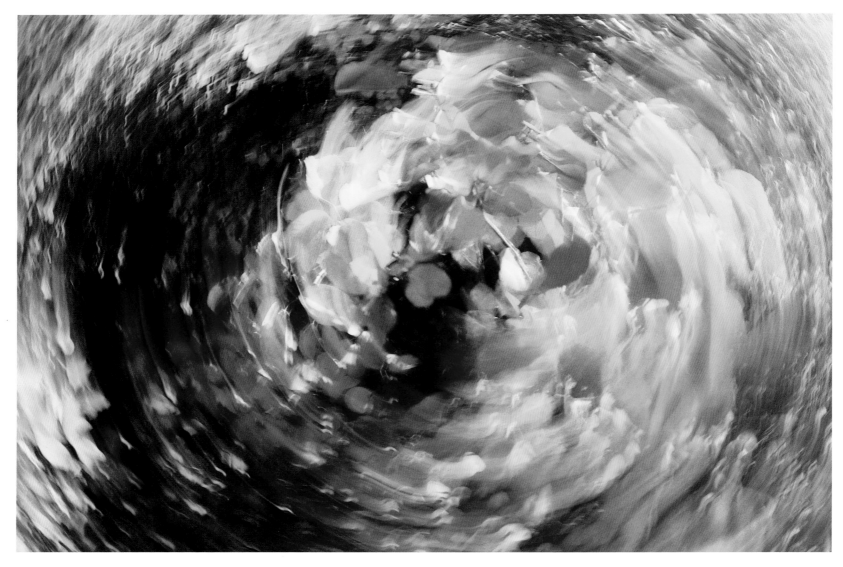

Camera motion on autumn foliage, near Saskatoon, SK, 1981

Multiple exposure of pine branches, Kananaskis Country, AB, 1988

Water reflection of sunset light on lake front, Wakaw Lake, SK, 1978

Sunrise on ice, near Saskatoon, SK, 1981

Wide angle of the rare jumped-up-green plant on active sand dune, Great Sandhills, SK, 1981

Closeup of morning dew on grasses, near Fish Creek, SK, 1981

Hoar frost on poplars, Grandora, SK, 1996

shimmering sunlight reflected on river with buffalo beans, near Saskatoon, SK, 1981

Shimmering sunlight reflected on river with closeup of budding aspen leaves, near Saskatoon, SK, 1981

Multiple exposure of poplars in autumn, Grandora, SK, 1996

Closeup of sand bar on S. Saskatchewan River, near Saskatoon, SK, 1981

Sandstone formation and morning light on clouds, Writing-On-Stone Provincial Park, AB, 1997

Closeup of caterpillar on a reed, Kingston, ON, 1982

"Next he made the critters.

"An' He got to thinkin', there ain't nobody fer to till this here soil, to one-way her, to drill her, ner to stook the crops, an' pitch the bundles, an' thrash her, when she's ripe fer thrashin', so He took Him some top soil — made her into the shape of a man — breathed down into the nose with the breath of life.

"That was Adam. He was a man.

"He set him down ontuh a section to the east in the districk a Eden — good land — lotsa water.

"The Lord stood back, an' He looked at what He done inside a one week an' she suited Him fine."

———————

WHO HAS SEEN THE WIND

Clydesdales on farm south of Weyburn, SK, 1998

Camera movement on man walking in front of brick wall, 1979

Harvesting at sunset on the Ray Milne farm, near Delisle, SK, 1997

Field of green wheat, near St. Isidore-de-Bellevue, SK, 1981

Canola field, Minichinas Hills, near Wakaw, SK, 1998

Stormy sky over rangeland, near Cereal, AB, 1998

Prairie

W. O. was born in 1914 in Weyburn, Saskatchewan. His own feelings about being raised on the prairies are described by one of his characters, Hugh, the seventy-year old narrator of *How I Spent My Summer Holidays*, who returns after many years to visit the prairie haunts of his childhood:

Now and as a child I walked out here to ultimate emptiness, and gazed to no sight destination at all. Here was the melodramatic part of the earth's skin that had stained me during my litmus years, fixing my inner and outer perspective, dictating the terms of the fragile identity contract I would have with myself for the rest of my life.

As a child, W.O. absorbed the wide spaces of the prairie, its dramatic shifts of light and shadow, its straight lines, and its salient signs of life and death. For the rest of his life he was marked by this landscape, emotionally and even, it seemed, physically. His face

stubble field in midday light, near Hanna, AB, 1998

was as transparently expressive as a field of wheat, bright and mobile in the wind, but as easily transformed by the shadow of clouds. His tousled hair always looked as wild as the prairie grasses. One of his school chums described him as having "no side." What he meant was that W.O. had a guilelessness that invited immediate friendship, an openness as wide as the prairie itself. There was nothing restrained about him; he was down-to-earth and irreverent. But he also had a darker streak, a profound sense of mortality and the passing of things, taught to him early on the prairies.

Who Has Seen the Wind opens with one of the most recognizable lines in Canadian literature: "Here was the least common denominator of nature, the skeleton requirements simply, of land and sky – Saskatchewan prairie." The mathematical metaphor catches not only the visual image of a landscape reduced to the bare minimum of sky, horizon line and land, it also suggests the skeletal destiny of humans. The novel depicts Brian's quest for answers to the basic, "skeleton" questions about birth and death. Visually precise and metaphorically suggestive though it is to Canadian eyes, this first line of the novel was considered dull and boring by W.O.'s American editor. When asked to remove it, W.O. argued that it expressed the "bareness of the prairie itself" and that it must stay in. There was, he thought, a distinction to be made between bareness and dullness. What W.O. saw was that the "ultimate emptiness" of the prairie was also "melodramatic."

And, for sensitive eyes and ears, there is variety in the seasonal changes to prairie, in its cloudscapes, in its wind voices. W.O. found as many ways to describe wind as the Inuit have found to describe snow. His sensibility, his philosophy of being, his aesthetics were all informed by this minimalist landscape which trained him to look closely and to listen acutely. In *Who Has Seen the Wind* he celebrates prairie landscape in rich lyrical prose and explores the growth of this way of seeing in his child protagonist, Brian. He called the prairie, and later the foothills, his "grass tower" (distinguishing it from the escapist "ivory tower"): "I had a grass tower childhood on the Saskatchewan prairies. Now I value the opportunity to stand still, to stare, to listen. You can do these things well in a grass tower. The listening is particularly important to a writer."

Looking up at sky and looking down at earth "you're in a world" says the Kid in *Jake and the Kid*, and "she's your own world." As a young boy W.O. and his friends had the whole prairie around Weyburn as their world, their grass tower. They hunted gophers, built underground caves, and swam in the Souris River — more a slow-moving creek with cattails spearing its mud banks — or skated on it in winter. The prairie sharpened his senses, and his prose is rich with what he called "sensuous fragments": the "stitching sound of grasshoppers," the "faint honey scent of wolf willow," the "escargot taste and smell" of the Souris, the meadowlark's "sudden bright notes splintering stillness." Even the no-sound of a hot mid-August noon is captured: "She was kind of numb out there, like the prairie bumped its funny bone." Like Joseph Conrad, one of his literary heroes, W.O. believed that the writer must appeal to his readers' senses, must strive through image and rhythm to make us touch, hear, smell, taste — above all to make us "see" our world.

In 1926, when W.O. was twelve, he developed bovine tuberculosis in his wrist, which prevented him from attending school on a regular basis. From 9:00 to 4:00, when all his friends were in school, he would go out onto the prairie and it felt, he said, as if "some great blackboard eraser had wiped all the children off all the streets — but missed me." He soon developed an introspectiveness beyond his years:

I would walk to the end of the street and out over the prairie with the clickety grasshoppers bunging in arcs ahead of me and I could hear the hum and twang of the wind in the great prairie harp of telephone wires. I remember looking down at the dried husk of a dead gopher crawling with ants and flies and undertaker beetles. Standing there with the total thrust of prairie sun on my vulnerable head, I guess I learned — at a very young age — that I was mortal.

(*An Evening with W.O. Mitchell*)

W.O. believed, as this passage indicates, that one's childhood landscape did more than imprint its physical geography; it also fixed an "inner perspective." He learned to see drama and poetry in small things, and he became acutely aware of his own separateness and his own mortality. Another prairie writer, Wallace Stegner, noted in *Wolf Willow* how prairie landscape affects you: "It is a country to breed mystical people, egocentric people, perhaps poetic people. But not humble ones. At noon the total sun pours on your single head; at sunrise or sunset you throw a shadow a hundred yards long. . . . Puny you may feel there, and vulnerable, but not unnoticed."

Who Has Seen the Wind is implicitly about "feeling" the force of the physical world. In 1946 when W.O. wrote to his American editor arguing that *Who Has Seen the Wind* had to end with the last two pages of prairie description, he explained that his description was not merely description but revealed a philosophic attitude. "I am not satisfied with a photographic realism. . . . [My] description of the prairie is not as objective as it may seem. . . ." The words and phrases in these last few pages show this clearly. He says "*seeking, truant*" were chosen deliberately. They say something about humans' constant seeking, questioning and defiant spirit. On the other hand, his descriptions of the "pigmy farm buildings" and of thunder as the "careless" sound of lumber being dropped are "all deliberate touches" that suggest fragility and vulnerability. The implications that man's structures are pigmy efforts and that Nature is "careless" are philosophic attitudes derived from his experiences as a young boy growing up on the prairie. His description of the "swarming hum" of "rime-white wires" on telephone poles stretching to the prairie's rim portray Brian's sense of linked family generations — a sense subtly reinforced in these last paragraphs which echo the repetition and rhythms of the book of Ecclesiastes. When he adapted the novel for television, W.O. chose those images that would "translate the prose description of 'the feeling' from interior to exterior visual." He wanted images of "bounding tumbleweed," of "summer fallow dust devils," of "moving cloud," and "the loneliest prairie sound of all — a metal sign clanking and swinging on an arm." The "prairie harp of telephone wires," he wrote, is "vaguely disturbing to any prairie child" because it says that "specific life is finite but that the abstract of prairie is forever and forever. It is the death motif." He worked hard at making his descriptive passages resonate emotionally, intellectually, and symbolically.

Prairie was a landscape that he could not remove from his imagination. His first twelve years on the prairies marked him indelibly, and he circled back to that landscape time and again, in his "Jake and the Kid" stories, in *How I Spent My Summer Holidays*, in the reminiscential performance pieces collected in *An Evening with W.O. Mitchell*, and in his last, unfinished novel.

W.O.'s work portrays a prairie world that has changed or disappeared. The upright miniature teepee-stooks of grain have been transformed into giant bread-loaf bales, the horse-drawn democrats have been replaced with four-wheel-drive trucks, and the dusty dirt ruts of Government Road are now a paved highway. Even the grain elevators which shouldered prairie town horizons are fast disappearing. Now the landscape is dotted with oil pumps, "metal birds tipping and sipping from deep in the earth." The hired man does not milk the cows in the quiet of the barn with only the sound of the "milk humming 'some-fun, some-fun,'" nor does he come home from the fields with the "jingle of the traces" of the horses' reins sounding "clear against the evening hush." The paint-box of prairie colours is now even more dramatic, with the intense yellow of canola overwhelming the subtler honey colour of ripened wheat. But some things remain the same. There are still the "skeleton requirements simply, of land and sky," there is still the sound of the wind "in the grass with a million timeless whisperings," and still the "faint honey scent of wolf willow [which] steals from river banks." The coyote "lifts his howl," the tiger lily blooms, the prairie crocus "opens blue," and the gopher "squeaks his impudence." Half a century after the writing of *Who Has Seen the Wind*, Courtney Milne's photographs capture these timeless elements: the drama of cloudscape, the seasonal extremes, the promise of harvest, the geometry of land and sky.

Here was the least common denominator of nature, the skeleton requirements simply, of land and sky – Saskatchewan prairie It lay wide around the town, stretching tan to the far line of the sky, clumped with low buck brush and wild rose bushes, shimmering under the late June sun and waiting for the unfailing visitation of wind, gentle at first, barely stroking the long grasses and giving them life; later, a long hot gusting that would lift the black top soil and pile it in barrow pits along the roads or in deep banks against the fences.

But for now, it was as though a magnificent breath were being held; stiff puffs of cloud were high in the sky, retaining their shapes for hours on end, one of them near the horizon, presenting a profile view of blown cheeks and extended lips like the wind personification upon an old map.

Over the prairie cattle stood still as the clouds, listless beside the dried-up slough beds which held no water for them. Where the snow white of alkali edged the course of the river, a thin trickle of water made its way toward the town low upon the horizon. Silver willow, heavy with dust, grew along the river banks, perfuming the air around with its honey smell.

Just before the town the river took a wide loop as though in search of some variation in the prairie's flat surface, found it in a deep-cut coulée ragged with underbrush, and entered the town at its eastern edge.

———————

WHO HAS SEEN THE WIND

Railroad crossing, near Tregarva, SK, 1998

Spring marsh, Wood Mountain Provincial Park, SK, 1995

Red samphire in alkali slough, near Batoche, SK, 1983

Granary and canola field, northwest of Meacham, SK, 1998

Country road, sunset light, northwest of Meacham, SK, 1998

CPR bridge and Souris River, Weyburn, SK, 1998

Even as I began to walk towards the river, I realized that I was on a time return. It was the same wind as the wind of my boyhood, still careless in the prairie grass, like the braided whisper that sighed restlessly through our classrooms. Maybe it wasn't the wind but the grasshoppers, stirred by my feet to leap ahead of me and drift sideways on the wind, that carried me with them in a memory loop back. . . .

———————

HOW I SPENT MY SUMMER HOLIDAYS

Souris River from canoe, Weyburn, SK, 1998

Morning sunlight on grounds of the "Mental Hospital," Weyburn, SK, 1998

I moved on through that anticipatory stillness, the wind constant at my cheek and nostrils, stirring my hair, till an old and familiar smell came to me. Wet potter's clay. I reached the river well upstream from the Mental Hospital powerhouse dam, where we had netted suckers in the spring. Here it was more long slough than river, phallic with cat-tails, frogs nudging their snouts and bump eyes through a green gruel of algae. As I walked along the Little Souris, I caught the smell of mint that was almost too perfect and then the perfume musk of wolf willow.

HOW I SPENT MY SUMMER HOLIDAYS

Rusted barrel and cattails, sunset light, Souris River, Weyburn, SK, 1998

Wide angle of Souris River from canoe, Weyburn, SK, 1998

Most important to me and the others in our child world was the Little Souris River, a wandering prairie vein, dark with earth flour, rushing and swollen with snow run-off in early spring, shrinking and slowing almost to stillness by mid-August. The river was ours, though it did seem undeserved, almost a miracle; for we knew that water ought to be earned by digging a well to find it, or a dug-out to capture it. In all seasons we were drawn to the river, less often for skating in winter, almost daily to swim during our summer holidays. Sundays — never.

———

HOW I SPENT MY SUMMER HOLIDAYS

Hockey game on pond ice, near Saskatoon, SK, 1980

Gumweed, Wanuskewin Heritage Park, Saskatoon, SK, 1991

All summer, we watched the sky, and whenever our wheat needed rain, the popcorn clouds got out of the way for the fat, grey-bellied ones that knew how to rain. Halfway through August she really got hot. Hot and still. So still the gophers squeaking sounded not right – like people whispering in Church. . . .

───────

"Elbow Room," ACCORDING TO JAKE AND THE KID

Late afternoon sky, Grandora, SK, 1998

Granaries, near Alvena, SK, 1981

I'd been lying on my stomach . . . and I'd rolled over onto my back to get a good look at the sky. There was Jake above me, looking down. And that was when I asked him. I asked him how much bluing she took to get prairie sky anyway.

"There ain't enough to do her," Jake said. "All the bluing on God's green earth won't do her."

———————

"Women Is Humans," JAKE AND THE KID

Horse on hillside, near Consul, SK, 1981

She was a funny sky, full of cloud stuff that went black along the horizon. Over top of us Somebody had stuck Their finger through, and yanked one long, ragged blue rip in her.

She was real still in all that empty prairie, lonely still. Every once in a while, in the high grass, the wind took a notion to whisper some but not like she really meant to. A meadowlark dropped some of his notes off a straw stack; the prairie quiet grabbed them up like a blotter does ink. She wasn't letting anything spoil her quiet.

I guess I'm not so fussy about the prairie when she's still before a rain; she's too much like in school like when Miss Henchbaw looks up, and you don't know who's in for it — before-the-strap quiet.

———

"Gettin' Born," ACCORDING TO JAKE AND THE KID

Farmhouse and sunset sky near St. Denis, SK, 1981

Full moon and clouds, night sky, Saskatoon, SK, 1988

She'd let up raining, and the sky wasn't dark any more. Behind some torn black cloud I could see a big, pale, tiddly-wink moon. Like they do after a rain storm, frogs way off in the night were singing in their sloughs. The air smelled cool and washed.

———————

"Gettin' Born," ACCORDING TO JAKE AND THE KID

Full moon and cloud, night sky, Saskatoon, SK, 1988

He looked up to find that the street had stopped. Ahead lay the sudden emptiness of the prairie. For the first time in his four years of life, other than visits to his Uncle Sean's farm, he was on the prairie.

He had seen it often, from the verandah of his uncle's farm-house, or at the end of a long street, but till now he had never heard it. The hollowing hum of telephone wires along the road, the ring of hidden crickets, the stitching sound of grasshoppers, the sudden relief of a meadow lark's song, were deliciously strange to him.

Without hesitation he crossed the road and walked out through the hip-deep grass stirring in the steady wind; the grass clung at his legs; haloed fox-tails bowed before him; looping grasshoppers sprang from hidden places in the grass, clicketing ahead of him to disappear then lift again.

WHO HAS SEEN THE WIND

Sunset sky, near Youngstown, SK, 1998

Grasshopper and setting sun, near Weyburn, SK, 1998

Closeup of dragonfly, near Kingston, ON, 1982

Water droplets on leaf, Emma Lake, SK, 1983

A twinkling of light caught his eye, and he turned his head to see that the new flake leaves of the spirea were starred in the sunshine; on every leaf were drops that had gathered during the night. He got up. They lay limpid, cradled in the curve of the leaves, each with a dark lip of shadow under its curving side and a star's cold light in its pure heart. As he bent more closely over one, he saw the veins of the leaf blown up under the drop's perfect crystal curve. The barest breath of a wind stirred at his face, and its caress was part of the strange enchantment too.

———

WHO HAS SEEN THE WIND

Closeup of sunflower with bee, near Saskatoon, SK, 1984

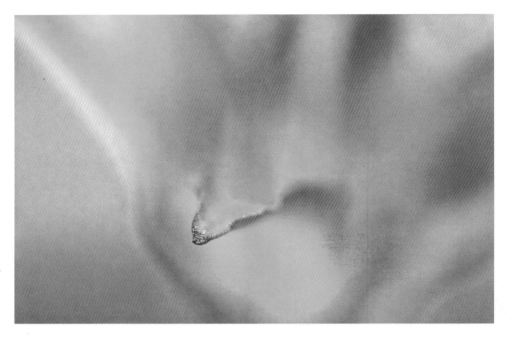

Closeup of prairie lily, near Saskatoon, SK, 1984

Within him something was opening, releasing shyly as the petals of a flower open, with such gradualness that he was hardly aware of it. But it was happening, an alchemy imperceptible as the morning wind, a growing elation of such fleeting delicacy and poignancy that he dared not turn his mind to it for fear that he might spoil it, that it might be carried away as lightly as one strand of spider web on a sigh of a wind. He was filled with breathlessness and expectancy, as though he was going to be given something, as though he was about to find something.

———

WHO HAS SEEN THE WIND

Sunrise, near Saltcoats, SK, 1997

The tailless gopher lay upon an ant pile, strangely still with the black bits of ants active over it. A cloud of flies lifted from it, dispersed, then came together again as at one command. Brian stared down at the two rodent teeth, the blood that had run down the nose and crusted there; he saw a short stump of tail skeleton with a ragged tab of skin that had stayed with the body when Ike had ripped away the tail. It was difficult to believe that this thing had once been a gopher that ran and squeaked over the prairie. It was difficult to believe that this was anything but dirt. . . .

The feeling was in Brian now, fierce — uncontrollably so with wild and unbidden power, with a new frightening quality. . . .

Prairie's awful, thought Brian, and in his mind there loomed vaguely fearful images of a still and brooding spirit, a quiescent power unsmiling from everlasting to everlasting to which the coming and passing of the prairie's creatures was but incidental. He looked out over the spreading land under intensely blue sky.

———————

WHO HAS SEEN THE WIND

Pile of deer skulls and antlers, farmyard near Fox Valley, SK, 1984

Cow skulls on farm gate, near Val Marie, SK, 1986

Time exposure of cloud passing over moon, near Milk River, AB, 1995

"It's going to storm, Sammy!" shouted Brian.

A tumble-weed went bounding past the boy and the old man, caught itself against the strands of the fence, then, released, went rolling on its way. An unnatural dusk that had grown over the whole prairie made Brian strain his eyes to see through the spread darkness of dust licked up by the wind in its course across the land. His ears were filled with the sound of the wind, singing fierce and lost and lonely, rising and rising again, shearing high and higher still, singing vibrance in a void, forever and forever wild.

As far as the two could see, the grasses lay flat to the prairie earth, like ears laid along a jack rabbit's back. They could feel the wind solid against their chests, solid as the push of a hand. It had plastered Sammy's beard around his cheek. Brian felt it sting his face with dust and snatch at his very breath. He was filled again with that ringing awareness of himself that he had experienced so often before.

―――――――

WHO HAS SEEN THE WIND

Tumbleweed in fence and blowing dust, near Dundurn, SK, 1980

Setting sun, south of Cupar, SK, 1998

Shadows lengthen; the sunlight fades from cloud to cloud, kindling their torn edges as it dies from softness to softness down the prairie sky. A lone farmhouse window briefly blazes; the prairie bathes in mellower, yellower light and the sinking sun becomes a low and golden glowing, splendid on the prairie's edge. . . . Stooks, fences, horses, man, have clarity that was not theirs throughout the day.

———————

WHO HAS SEEN THE WIND

Mare and newborn foal, sunset light, Saskatoon, SK, 1980

He reached the straw stack and felt it clammy with night dampness. He began to dig, and when he had a hole cleared out, climbed in and pulled the straw about himself. Lying there he looked up to the dark face of the sky pricked out with stars. He was filled now with a feeling of nakedeness and vulnerability that terrified him. As the wind mounted in intensity so too the feeling of defencelessness rose in him. It was as though he listened to the drearing wind and in the spread darkness of the prairie night was being drained of his very self. He was trying to hold together something within himself, that the wind demanded and was relentlessly leeching from him.

———————

WHO HAS SEEN THE WIND

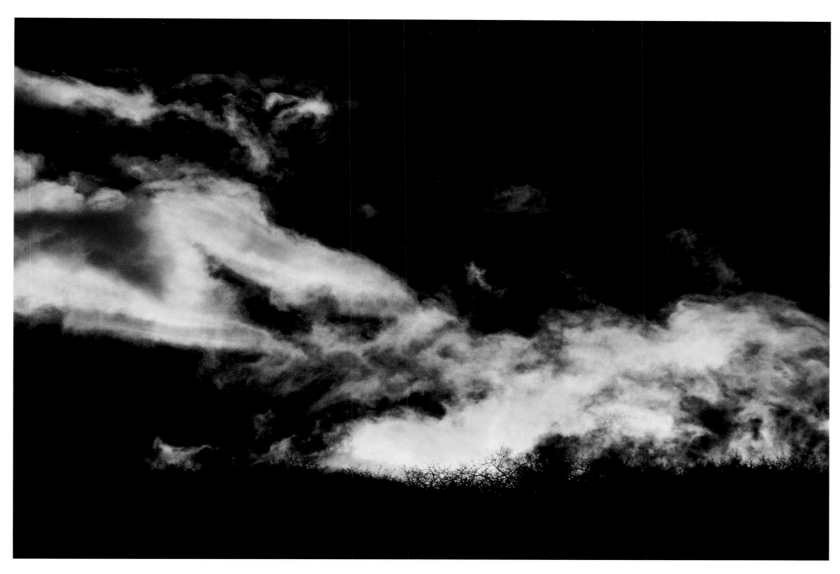

Light refraction in clouds at sunset, near Carway, AB, 1997

Grain elevators and night sky, Saskatchewan, 1980

Just as he reached the road the sun exploded softly over the prairie's eastern edge, its long, red fingers discovering the clouds curved down the prairie sky. He began to walk along the road at the end of which he could now see the sloping shoulders of the town's grain elevators.

———————

WHO HAS SEEN THE WIND

Grain elevators, Saskatchewan, 1980

Thistles in ditch and abandoned farm, near Marquis, SK, 1998

Fall brought another crop failure to the district; the land was dotted now with empty farmhouses, their blank windows staring out over the spreading prairie, their walls piled high with rippled banks of black dust; farmers and their families moved westward and northward to Alberta and the Peace River country. Freights were dotted with unemployed, many of them young boys who had never had jobs in their lives. . . .

The town showed the depression; houses needed paint; cars on Main Street on Saturday evenings were older models; plate glass windows were empty where businesses had left. . . .

—————————

WHO HAS SEEN THE WIND

Boys' and girls' outhouses in abandoned schoolyard, south of Mankota, SK, 1986

Abandoned farmhouse and water wagon, west of Lacadena, SK, 1992

Geese at Wood River, near Lafleche, SK, 1995

Interior of abandoned house, northwest of Regina, SK, 1998

Closeup of truck fender, farmyard near Fox Valley, SK, 1984

Front of machine shed, farmyard near Fox Valley, SK, 1984

Steer skulls on barn wall, farmyard near Fox Valley, SK, 1984

Store front, Fox Valley, SK, 1984

The rest of the way home we just rolled along with the buckboard wheels sort of grinding. A gopher squeaked a couple of times. The way it is in fall, the air was just like soda pop. Every once in a while would come a tickle to your nose or forehead, and you would brush at it, only it would keep right on tickling. You couldn't see the spider webs floating on the air, except where sunshine caught onto them and slid down.

———

"The Liar Hunter," JAKE AND THE KID

Wagon wheels and sage, farmyard near Fox Valley, SK, 1984

Concrete barn built by Jim Mitchell, W.O. Mitchell's uncle, near Weyburn, SK, 1998

The boys dived into the barn's dusk, soothed with the richness of horse smell, dry with the sweetness of hay. There between the long lines of dropped tails, they waited for their eyes to become accustomed to the dimness. Here and there, Brian saw the turned head of a horse with white gleaming wild at the corner of its eyes. . . .

Brian could hear the wind sighing gently at the chinking in the barn walls . . . the regular grinding of horses at their oats, now and then the indifferent swish of a tail, the imperative knock of a hoof.

WHO HAS SEEN THE WIND

Closeup of nail shadows on Mitchell barn door, near Weyburn, SK, 1998

Spider and web, Good Spirit Provincial Park, SK, 1998

sunlight through roof boards, fisheye lens, farmhouse, SK, 1995

Closeup of plum tree after October blizzard, Saskatoon, SK, 1984

The black branches of the trees along Sixth Street were edged with white, the staring white that belongs to a child's paint box. Feathering lazily, crazily down, loosed from the hazed softness of the sky, the snow came to rest in startling white bulbs on the dead leaves of the poplars, webbing in between the branches. Just outside the grandmother's room, where she lay quite still in her bed, the snow, falling soundlessly, flake by flake piled up its careless weight. Now and again a twig would break off suddenly, relieve itself of a white burden of snow, and drop to earth.

———————

WHO HAS SEEN THE WIND

Blanket on clothesline after unexpected October blizzard, Saskatoon, SK, 1984

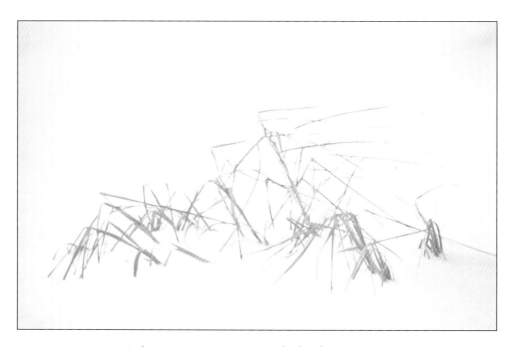

Windswept grasses in snow, south of Saskatoon, SK, 1981

By the time that school was over that afternoon, the wind, gathering strength over the prairie where the sky over the horizon was dark and forbidding, swept down upon the town, throating wildly, tossing the black branches of their poplars, lifting the loose snow and driving it into the children's faces, stinging their eyes and noses above the scarves tied round their mouths. Brian tasted the coldness of it with each breath, a clinging sensation at the back of his throat and in his nostrils — like the touch of an icicle to a bare hand.

———————

WHO HAS SEEN THE WIND

Highway in January blizzard, near Biggar, SK, 1997

Light snowfall on tilled field, near Arelee, SK, 1980

Goose-grey above him, the prairie sky had a depthless softness undetermined by its usual pencil edge, melting invisibly into the spread and staring white of the land. He walked over the prairie, his ankles turning to the frozen crust of hummocking summer fallow and stubble fields. No living thing moved; and he saw only the domino tracks of jack rabbits, the sidling wells of a trotting coyote's trail, the exquisitely stamped tracks of prairie chicken. These things filled his mind against his will.

WHO HAS SEEN THE WIND

Crusted snowdrifts and afternoon sun, near Aberdeen, SK, 1981

Wild rye grass in snow, south of Saskatoon, SK, 1981

All kinds of people had died. They were dead and they were gone. The swarming hum of telephone wires came to him, barely perceptible in the stillness, hardly a sound heard so much as a pulsing of power felt. He looked up at rime-white wires, following them from pole to pole to the prairie's rim. From each person stretched back a long line — hundreds and hundreds of years — each person stuck up.

———

WHO HAS SEEN THE WIND

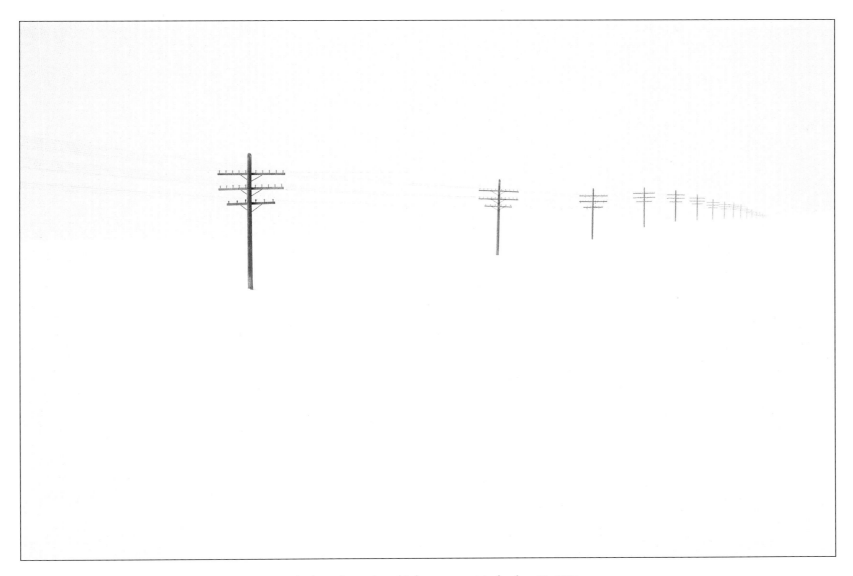

Telephone lines along highway, near Kindersley, SK, 1977

sunrise light on snow-laden birch, Grandora, SK, 1996

Spring came to the prairie with the suddenness of a meadow lark's song. Overnight the sky traded its winter tang for softness; the snow already honey-combed with the growing heat of a closer sun, melted — first from the steaming fallow fields, then the stubble stretches, shrinking finally to uneven patches of white lingering in the barrow pits. Here and there meadow larks were suddenly upon straw stacks, telephone wires, fence posts, their song clear with ineffable exuberance that startled and deepened the prairie silence — each quick and impudent climax of notes leaving behind it a vaster, emptier, prairie world.

WHO HAS SEEN THE WIND

Melting frost on crabapple tree, Grandora, SK, 1995

Melting lake ice on shoreline, 1997

First crocuses of the season, near Clavet, SK, 1996

Spring melt on tilled field, near Cudworth, SK, 1996

Spring melt on slough, near Cudworth, SK, 1996

Sage, rock, and coulee, the Bear Hills, north of Perdue, SK, 1998

[**I**'m] fussy about Mac's coulee in spring. Here's how she is:

    Still, still as water, with the sun coming kind of streaky through the wolf willow along her edges — what you might call stiff sunlight the way she's full of dust dancing all along her. And when you lie on your belly at the bottom of Mac's coulee, you're in a world; she's your own world, and there's nobody else there, and you can do what you want with her.

———————

JAKE AND THE KID

Setting sun and melting snow on field, Grandora, SK, 1997

Spring green on field, from hilltop south of Rockglen, SK, 1983

Under the distinctly pencilled edge of the chinook arch, the sky was ideal blue. Crows called; farmers, impatient as though it was the only spring left in the world to them, burning with the hope that this one would not be another dry year, walked out to their implements, looked over them and planned their seeding — barley here, oats there, wheat there, summer fallow there.

In town the trees' branches fattened into sticky buds. Geese flew overhead at night in wavering vee's, their far-off calls drifting down.

———

WHO HAS SEEN THE WIND

Farm road and granaries south of Rockglen, SK, 1983

Snow melt on field, near Swift Current, SK, 1981

Riding home in the democrat with Ma and Jake, I didn't do so much thinking. When she's spring it isn't so easy for a person to think anything but goofy thoughts — like wondering what she'd be like to bounce off clouds. Over top of us the sky was what you might call a luke-blue. All alongside the road the fields were green with new wheat. There isn't any green like young wheat green stretching out spang to the horizon, bright green like to yell at a person.

———————

"Gettin' Born," ACCORDING TO JAKE AND THE KID

Green wheat in afternoon light, near St. Isadore-de-Bellevue, SK, 1981

Swathed field, near Weyburn, SK, 1998

That age and the isolated rural village of my boyhood are long, long gone. Our town lay in the South Saskatchewan prairies, sixty miles north of the Montana border. The superlative sun that shone down on us was Greek; the grass sea around us was our Aegean.

―――――

HOW I SPENT MY SUMMER HOLIDAYS

Camera motion on windswept grasses, near Central Butte, SK, 1983

Straw bales in sunset light, east of Beiseker, AB, 1998

As he turned back toward the town he saw the moon pale in the afternoon sky, a grey ghost half-dissolved. And the town was dim – grey and low upon the horizon, it lay, not real, swathed in bodiless mists – quite sunless in the rest of the dazzling prairie.

WHO HAS SEEN THE WIND

Grain elevator in sunset light at Beadle, near Kindersley, SK, 1998

View from Highway 7, West of High River, AB, 1998

Foothills & Mountains

W. O. went on to live in other landscapes and, chameleon-like, he absorbed their colours, but he never lost the imprint of his first twelve years on the prairie. At age thirteen he moved to California for the winter, and for the following three years he went to high school in St. Petersburg, Florida. His sub-tropical experiences in his adolescent years made him forever desire tropical warmth, earth smell and orchid pleasure in his environment. He added a greenhouse and solarium to his High River and Calgary houses so that he could raise orchids, birds of paradise, and cut-leaf palms to give some reprieve from what he called the "stun" of foothill winters.

High River, Alberta, where he settled with Merna and their two boys in 1945, was softer and greener than the Saskatchewan prairies, but it too spoke a "poetry of earth" and was "the right place in which to write and to raise children." It was here that he took up fly fishing and shotgunning with a passion that amused his neighbours but at times dismayed Merna. W.O. had no sense of time while out in the field or on the river, and he

View from Highway 7, west of High River, AB, 1998

111

often had to make up for it by typing late into the night to meet a deadline – while Merna tried to sleep. His love of fishing and hunting grew as much out of his delight in foothills "poetry" as it did out of the atavistic excitement of the hunt. He introduced his sons to fishing and hunting, but hoped they would find more in these pastimes than simple sport, that they too would find a way of seeing and being:

> I think my older son found it last summer [1954] . . . not on the prairie but along a foothills stream. There he cast again and again the gray hackle fly he had tied for himself. Rings slowly widened and spread to grassy banks. Sunlight disced and danced on shaded water; clear bubbles and foam were borne slowly circling past him; mosquitoes whined thin and he had broken off for himself a warm and humming fragment of August. I think the poetry of earth is real for him now.

To the east of High River he could see the familiar prairie flatness, but to the west was the slight rise of the tan foothills and then the blue ridges of the Rocky Mountains, often appearing much closer, in the clear mountain air, than their thirty miles' distance would suggest. He never got over "the lift" they gave him. Still, he saw them with prairie eyes and their everlasting presence stirred contradictory responses: "they comforted, yet they surprised at the same time."

He made a point of learning about the country at the foot of the eastern slopes of the Rockies when he was writing "The Alien" from 1952-54. He moved a trailer out to Eden Valley and there lived and taught on the Stoney Indian reserve, which is just at the entrance to the Kananaskis area, now a tourist destination. He fished the Eden Valley stretches of the Highwood River up to the first forest-range cattle guard and beyond to a five-mile stretch of the Highwood known then as "the canyon." He and Merna occasionally helped with the fall round-up and brandings in the Eden Valley and one year, as research for the novel that became *Since Daisy Creek*, he went on a grizzly bear hunt in the early spring, not with a gun but with a pencil! Riding into the mountains by horseback he got to know some of the higher reaches and mountain valleys at close range. In his Alberta books he found as many ways to describe mountains, chinook skies, foothills, and fast-moving mountain rivers as he had the "bald-headed" prairie and the prairie winds. He gave

Rockies and foothills from hilltop, northwest of Longview, AB, 1998

character to this landscape in "The Alien," *The Kite, The Vanishing Point, Since Daisy Creek*, and *Roses Are Difficult Here*. Many of the "Jake and the Kid" stories were written in High River, and although the mythical town of Crocus is firmly located in Saskatchewan prairie, Mitchell claimed that "one out of five parts" of Crocus was High River.

In 1948 he moved his family to Toronto where he became fiction editor at *Maclean's*. Although this was a stimulating environment in which to live and work, Merna and W.O. decided to return to High River three years later. His friend Pierre Berton took bets with all of the *Maclean's* staff that Mitchell would not last more than six months in the little cowtown in the foothills — that he would be creatively and intellectually starved without the excitement of the Toronto writing community in which he had become caught up. Another friend accused him of "fleeing to the ivory tower:"

> He said that the world was in a state of upheaval, that it was selfish of me, that my social and artistic conscience must be pretty well numbed, if I could even contemplate leaving Toronto and deliberately burying myself among or in or under tobacco chewing characters who had never reclined on a psychiatrist's couch, heard of Christopher Fry, existentialism, CBC WEDNESDAY NIGHT. He was wrong on almost every count.

But it was not a flight — and W.O. was not going to an ivory tower but to a "grass tower." In order to write he needed earth and sky. He wanted to see "wild ducks assaulting the sky in morning and evening flight, the lick and spit of an August lawn sprinkler, a wild canary in the hedge, the faint mucous trail of a snail on a leaf." He needed to again hear the "voices" of the people and country he wrote about.

W.O. and Merna moved to Calgary in 1968 and his later novels reflect the city life and the university community in which he lived, not just in Calgary, but in a number of other locations, including Edmonton, Toronto, and Windsor. But he always sought out what he called "the green element," even in the city. His permanent home in Calgary was directly across from a treed park and lay only half a block from the Elbow River. He also had two rural retreats that met his need for the green element. He never used his cottage in the Shuswap area of B.C. as a setting for a novel, but he spent nearly every summer there from

1961 until the early 1990s. There he had his yearly rendezvous with rainbow trout and chinook salmon in Mabel Lake and the Shuswap River. He set his typewriter up on the cabin deck but, in fact, did most of his summer writing in his head as he fished the same waters as the resident ospreys and watched the wind play over the lake's surface, surrounded by fir trees and low tree-covered mountains. Nearer Calgary he had a retreat on the Dog Pound Creek, north of Cochrane, where he occasionally fished for brown trout and pike. In his last novel, *For Art's Sake*, the hero turns for release from city and university life to the green element of the Dog Pound's foothills.

W.O. took a possessive interest in whatever landscape he lived in, responding enthusiastically to its "poetry" and praising its various and unique characteristics. Even in Windsor or Toronto this prairie boy found something remarkable. Two places, though, claimed him more than any others. High River was "special" for him, a place he loved at first sight. It was, he wrote in an article in 1962, "a town with a conservative personality, which makes you love her and lose patience with her, but it is still a cow town taking its rhythms from the seasons." And Weyburn prairie was his first and most enduring love.

View of foothills from high hill northeast of Longview, AB, 1988

The softly lifting foothills in which High River lay, did not possess the starkness of Saskatchewan prairie spread to a far horizon; always to the West there were the Rockies, withdrawn, cool and abiding, immutable rock and glacier that drew the eye and held it steadily till the sight was sated. Poplar and cottonwood protected streets and lawns, softening and clothing with a shade denied to naked prairie towns.

To the East of the town lay wheat farms; to the West, the ranches sprawled to the forest reserve in the mountains beyond.

———

THE ALIEN

View looking west to high hill, northeast of Longview, AB, 1998

Autumn in the Eden Valley, west of Longview, AB, 1998

It was fall when I saw High River for the first time; the foothills' air had the wild tang that first frost gives to apples, turnips and children playing Red Light under street lamps. . . . Cottonwood trees along the streets had turned to an amber so luminous in the September sun that a person walking under them felt he was seeing their colour through his forehead.

———————

MY HOME TOWN: HIGH RIVER

Autumn in the Qu'Appelle Valley, south of Southey, SK, 1997

Over the swathed fields spreading out from Shelby, devouring combines rolled with their wide mouths low before themselves. The men did not harvest alone, for sharp-tailed grouse lifted over them in chittering flight, occasional partridge coveys fluttered and planed, and crimson-eyed pheasant cocks, with bronze breasts distended, moved up out of the coulees and the river banks to strut through the ripe grain. From potholes, reedy sloughs, and river backwaters came the ticket-ticket confidences, the fully derisive quack of whole communities of ducks; on sibilant wings they launched their punctual assault against the dawn and sunset skies. Daily they welcomed the splashing arrival of each new contingent of pintail, mallard, and canvas-back from the North. Thread after thread of snow geese unravelled from the far horizon, grew loud and shrill as they circled over Cooper's Lake, broke formation, then, still calling, fell like snowflakes through the sun.

ROSES ARE DIFFICULT HERE

Sunset over Cooper's Point, Frank Lake, near High River, AB, 1998

Pond at the Paint Pots, Banff National Park, AB, 1998

Autumn grasses and algae, Frank Lake, near High River, AB, 1998

Autumn colour, Frank Lake, near High River, AB, 1998

Autumn colour, Frank Lake, near High River, AB, 1998

August marsh colours, northwest of Regina, SK, 1998

To the North ran a tan and green line of hills bunched with buckbrush, for all the world like the clump bodies of buffalo at a distance, fixed in the act of grazing.

———

THE ALIEN

Qu'Appelle Valley from junction of Highways 6 and 99, northeast of Craven, SK, 1998

Discs of light from reflection on Highwood River, AB, 1998

He turned the swivel chair to face himself and sat down in it. Whenever he had been blocked in his writing, he had so often found escape in tying flies. It seemed to anaesthetize failure pain for him. As loose feathers stirred and lifted and drifted over the desk-top under his gentle breathing, and one by one the flies were freed from the vise to rest high upon their hackle tips, his tension would loosen more and more to release his mind and his imagination. In this basement cave he could forget that winter stunned outside. Down here sunlight disced and danced on water; river rings slowly widened and spread to grassy banks; foam and bubbles were borne circling by; grasshoppers leaped clicketing; mosquitos whined; blue darning needles darted, held, and darted on again in their capricious flight.

SINCE DAISY CREEK

W.O.'s snuff box and early typewriter, Calgary, AB, 1998

In his six Shelby High River years he had not yet got over the lift he got at each new sight of the Rockies, and doubted that he ever would; he seldom entered the newspaper office without a last glance in their direction, and many mornings he went to the door simply to look at them. It was not so much the first ridge of the foothills and its shadowed darkness that appealed, but the more remote range, snow-covered summer and winter, checked with dark draws, its purity complete reflection of all light. . . .

He came to the overgrown ruts of the river road winding through cottonwood, willow, and saskatoon; the coolness of shade closed round him. For a moment he stood still, striving to catch the hoarse pulse of the river. He heard it faintly; with a quick thrill of anticipation he walked on, holding the rod tip out ahead.

The sound of the river was full in his ears now as he crossed open grass to the shale and rock of the river bank. The water was high, and though it was not so murky as he had thought it might be, he knew that a dry fly would be useless. Above him the stream, frothing deep through rock, fell with a thumping roar into the spreading pool below, where foam and spray anguish ended abruptly in slick water slowly eddying.

——————

ROSES ARE DIFFICULT HERE

Highwood River, from George Lane Park, High River, AB, 1998

First light on Rockies, from Highway 5 near Cardston, AB, 1997

Sunrise on Rockies, from Highway 5 near Cardston, AB, 1997

Lower Falls, Johnston Canyon, Banff National Park, AB, 1998

Lower Falls from cave, Johnston Canyon, Banff National Park, AB, 1998

Shoreline of Highwood River, George Lane Park, High River, AB, 1998

Meadow, at turnoff to Kananaskis Lakes, Peter Lougheed Provincial Park, Ab, 1998

Once more he was looking down on water mirror, reflecting wolf willow silver along its edge. Over there the spear green of bull rushes. The pond's mud margin held deep hoof pocks where Hutterian cattle had come down to drink.

He was startled by a frog plop. The water surface was creased with the lilliputian wake of a water bug moving in minute epilepsy. Stopped. Held still. Twitched on again over pure surface.

He knelt and began to unlace his shoes. Perhaps the pond could wash sorrow away. With mild chill it embraced him; he pulled himself down and through the cool underwater murk, then arching broke the surface to expel pent breath and spray. He lay floating with the sting of pond water in his nostrils, the flat earth taste of it at the back of his mouth and throat. As though not part of him his hands fluttered at his sides; his knees moved lazily and unbidden as he stared up to sky and still cloud. Diluted by cool and fluid intimacy of water on nakedness, the tension flowed slowly from him.

———————

FOR ART'S SAKE

Pond at the Paint Pots, Banff National Park, AB, 1998

Barnyard at Dog Pound, northwest of Cochrane, AB, 1998

Water reflection of spring blossoms, Vancouver, BC, 1997

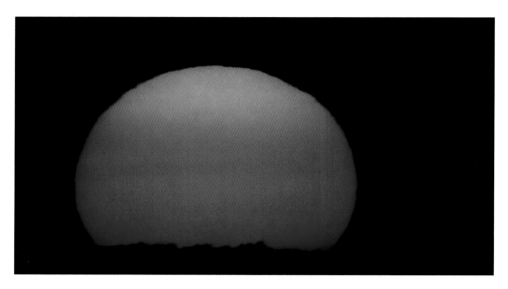

Setting sun with 3000mm lens, near Aberdeen, SK, 1987

So it was in a fuller and mellower light that Jacob walked home. The rayless sun slipped behind the white ridges of the mountains just as he reached the river crossing; the dark streaking clouds above were flushed with soft pink and salmon; they became swiftly ruby, and in a moment the entire sky had become a bloody and a hellish thing. The rippled surface of the river caught the red gleaming; the hills themselves became crimson. Jacob thought of men's faces florid at the mouth of John, the Blacksmith's forge; he thought of hell and roasting souls, and the Preacher's voice came to him:

"And I will show you wonders in heaven and in earth, blood and fire and pillars of smoke." To the east he saw the straight lifting smoke from burning straw stacks. "The sun shall be turned into darkness, and the moon into blood, before the great and terrible day of the Lord come."

———————

THE DEVIL'S INSTRUMENT

Sunrise sky, near Elrose, SK, 1992

Mt. Assiniboine, Mt. Assiniboine Provincial Park, BC, 1998

Now the highway arrowed north so that the mountains lifted to his left with such superlative clarity it was hard to believe they were all of forty miles away. They comforted, yet they surprised at the same time. Was it because he'd been a prairie child? Today they seemed special – reassuring in their abiding presence – daubed with white almost thick against the blue. They looked just the way a child with a paint box would want his mountains to turn out. . . .

When he was a boy, mountains had worried him slightly; at eight or nine he'd wondered how they ever got their railroad engines and passenger and freight coaches up the steep sides and over the tops and down the other sides of them.

THE VANISHING POINT

Snow-covered range from trail to Wonder Pass, Mt. Assiniboine Provincial Park, BC, 1998

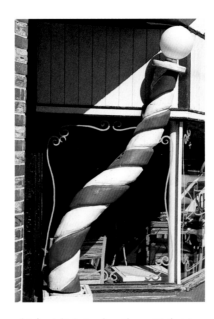

Frontage of Schmidty's Barber Shop, High River, AB, 1998

He made the right turn onto Johnston Trail, and they began the shallow descent into the city's heart. Far ahead, the Devonian Tower thrust with stiff arrogance fully a third higher than the tallest of the office buildings around; from the broad cylindrical base the concave slope sides soared six hundred feet, so that its glass revolving restaurant, boutiques, gift shop, broadcasting station, CSFA, floated above traffic smog. Pretty nearly the only six-hundred-foot concrete erection in the British Commonwealth. With a May basket balanced on its tip — that twinkled with coloured lights at night. North America. And had a red oil derrick to spear the last fifty feet.

———

THE VANISHING POINT

Multiple exposure of night lights of downtown Calgary, AB, 1998

Highwood River and autumn colour, Eden Valley, AB, 1998

Out on the Anchor P not so much has changed [since the 1880s]. The tan Buffalo grass on the ranges splashed with apple-green and the yellow cottonwood, the far hills hazed lavender and russet with wild rose haws and buckbrush turning, the flat, clear lift of the Rockies pulled into sharp wrinkled peaks, these have not changed.

It is Indian summer now in the foothills where the cottonwood is yellow touched up with high green, and the Rockies stand flat and distant against the sky.

COW HEAVEN

Mountain ridge from the Smith Dorrien-Spray Trail, Kananaskis Provincial Park, AB, 1998

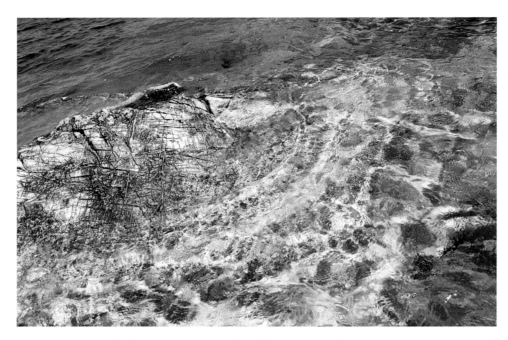

Shallow water over rock, Lake Minnewanka, AB, 1998

Their descent took them within sight of the river. It was no longer the wide and smooth flowing river they had known to the East. They caught glimpses of its narrow ribbon the glacial green of all mountain streams, deep between the chasm of hundred foot cut banks of grey rock and shale. Whole tortured stretches of it were milky below them. . . .

They walked over the open field, came to the cliff edge of the river; before they had reached it the roar of the falls had begun to hush their ears. They looked down to a tarn-like pool below; just above, the river flowed over a shelf, to drop in an anguished web of mist and spray.

————————

THE ALIEN

Johnston Canyon, Banff National Park, AB, 1998

Mountain mist from Moose Meadow, Banff National Park, AB, 1998

At the head of the valley the true mountains stood, great glacial facts against the late afternoon sky, presenting first a vista of gloomy pine, then spined and rocky disorder streaked and fluted and barred with radiance. The head must lift for eyes to attain the sterile peaks gauzed with light cloud.

———

THE ALIEN

Morning cloud and spruce tree, from Harvie Heights, Canmore, AB, 1998

There was simply stillness mild with the diffused light of dawn, now and again clearly the call of one bird. The darkness imperceptibly thinned, the lifting mountain to the West taking to itself more solidity till it stood out a rocky elephantine brow against the growing luminosity of the sky. To the East the sheer rise of rock in jumbled and jagged profusion, materialized. . . .

The whole lake lay unawakened, innocent of ripple or stir, smoking with morning mist. With bolt upright neck, sedate upon glass water, a loon floated into view. And now the morning was woven with the sound of birds, their brightness inextricably mixed.

Reluctantly, lingeringly the last of the mist breathed from the face of the lake which reflected the sheer mountain side perfectly: the rust and tan and grey of the shale, the dark and sabering trees, the spruce and its porcupine. The reflection gave the illusion of incredible depth. . . .

———————

THE ALIEN

Victoria Glacier, from Chateau Lake Louise, Banff National Park, AB, 1998

Morning light on Cascade Mountain, from Vermilion Lakes, near Banff, AB, 1998

Morning mist on Mt. Rundle, from Vermilion Lakes, near Banff, AB, 1998

Sunrise light on Mt. Assiniboine from Lake Magog, Mt. Assiniboine Provincial Park, BC, 1998

Reflection of Mt. Assiniboine at shore of Lake Magog, Mt. Assiniboine Provincial Park, BC, 1998

Sunset light from trail to Wonder Pass, Assiniboine Valley, Mt. Assiniboine Provincial Park, BC, 1998

Autumn larch and sunset light, from trail to Wonder Pass, Assiniboine Valley, Mt. Assiniboine Provincial Park, BC, 1998

Johnston Creek at bottom of Johnston Canyon, Banff National Park, AB, 1998

Sanders came down almost weekly, and they coursed the stream-banks together, the back cast of their lines whispering high behind them. Taut line communication with fighting rainbow seemed enough for them; they seldom spoke to each other, each in his own solitude throughout the smooth mornings and afternoons. . . .

It was remarkable how the metronomic regularity of the fly rod back and forth, the rolling out of line and leader to drop the fly, the hours of reading the water surface, vacuumed the mind clean of the finest dust of thought. And when [Sinclair] took attention from the water, rocks and trees and opposite bank were no longer fixed. They drifted sideways, and he himself was part of the magic land flow — grassinclair — cloudsinclair — sinclairock. . . .

————

THE VANISHING POINT

Water reflection of birch and pine, near Lac La Ronge, SK, 1978

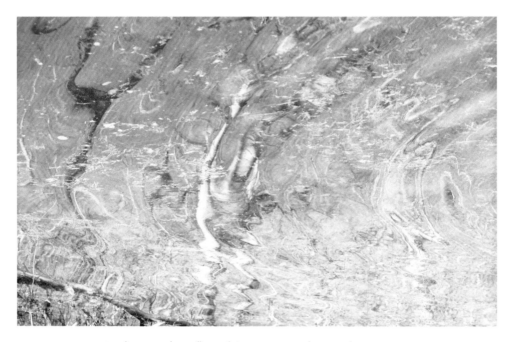

Poplar trunks reflected in water, Wakaw Lake, SK, 1978

The sound of the river seemed almost to have become part of him, like the pulse of his own blood in his ears; it dulled self-awareness, erased all tension; he thought vaguely of wild and religious men wandering through desert solitudes, conversing with a God Who made His Presence known to them. And in the roaring heart of the falls, half articulations chuckled and broke off just short of communication, hoarse and shrill conversations only dimly heard. He sat up and the opposite river bank with its willow and birch, drifted and wavered and ran before his eyes now used to the race and swirl of the stream.

———————

THE ALIEN

Johnston Creek at bottom of Johnston Canyon, Banff National Park, AB, 1998

And there was the canyon sound now, a deep chord, persistent, much more than wind sigh through leaf and needle branches. This hum was a master thrumming, as though Storm and Misty canyon's lofting sides formed a giant rock viola to give the wind a resin edge. When he had come in with Archie, he had thought this was a shaman place set aside from ordinary places. Here a hero could seek vision and solution so that he could lead his people out of want and danger. Here he could purify and prepare, and be absolved from self, and that was the great trick — the true magic — not to turn into an osprey or a falcon or an eagle or a magpie — but to fly free of self. This was the seed place where Esau had dreamed of leading his band, to find the happy days that they had lost.

Archie had told him that this was where Beulah began, flowing north. . . . They'd had to walk up the canyon a hundred yards to drink from it. It had made Carlyle's teeth ache. When he and Archie stood again, they could see up to the springs, a white water web down the rock face where the end of the canyon narrowed — was almost blind. The high sides there were bare of trees, the rock carved by millennia of wind and frost and water, suggesting the clump bodies of grazing buffalo, a bear, a goat, and unmistakably — a third of the way up the eastern wall — a demon face — witty — derisive.

THE VANISHING POINT

Rock face and creek at campground, Livingston Falls Provincial Recreation Area, AB, 1998

Late one afternoon, as he came down the river, he saw Esau Rider sitting on the rock slope at the foot of the suspension bridge. Third time he'd seen him there; the old man must spend many hours on that rock where the afternoon sun fell warmest. Carlyle stopped a hundred feet up stream to watch him, elbows on his knees, hands hanging loose. Possibly hours that way — stirring only to fill and light his pipe — staring down at the rock, where orange fungus scaled its minute foliage — or into the water where perhaps a bull trout hung. Esau-trout — trout-Esau. God, how he envied him his primitive talent for self-erasure, if it saved him from melancholy, from flesh and spirit pain. Did he achieve oneness with eternity? — what an overblown way to explain sun-warmed stupor in which half-thoughts and fragment dreams were projected against no time, lighted up, shaded and faded and vanished to light up again. Not too much different from the steers and cows with absently moving jaws — or the bull trout — or the fungus.

THE VANISHING POINT

Lichen on rock, Writing-On-Stone Provincial Park, AB, 1995

As he travelled he had been steadily climbing till finally the trail was merely a shaley ledge where the misstep of a horse meant tumbling death. Late in the afternoon he came upon the highest point of the pass and stopped there to wind his horses.

Below him as he stood, stretched an edgeless cloud sea. Within minutes a wind had risen, swirling and eddying mist, carding it apart to reveal first the peaks, then the mountain sides gloomy with dark pine, and finally the valley itself softly wraithed with the processional clearing. At length when the valley was free of mist, he saw it clearly, deep below himself, dignified with profound and tranquil emptiness. At his command, the sorrel tilted down; Carlyle leaned back against the cantle, the rope of the grey pack horse, jerking at his arm. Soon he was moving through closely congregating jack pine. He had reached the valley floor just at dusk. . . .

The sight of the familiar peak, without warning and so close, was a shock. The ploughsharing ridge had immediacy now, seemed almost near enough for one closing sprint of his horse to carry him right to its base.

———————

THE ALIEN

Afternoon cloud in Bow Valley, from Highway 1A, Banff National Park, AB, 1998

Morning mist in meadow at Lake Magog, Assiniboine Valley, Mt. Assiniboine Provincial Park, BC, 1998

Reflections of larch trees in Magog creek, Mt. Assiniboine Provincial Park, BC, 1998

Larch trees and snow on mountain, Naiset Point, Mt. Assiniboine Provincial Park, BC, 1998

Wide angle of rocks in Magog Creek, Mt. Assiniboine Provincial Park, BC, 1998

He was forced to walk and lead his horse, for the trail led straight into burnt over land – a seemingly endless maze of dead–fall with naked grey trunks tilting, tangled, lying flat, spotted throughout with the charred stumps of spruce, sable obscenities with even their raying roots checked and gleaming carbon black. The sight of them appalled him as had the cigarish harshness carried on the wind from the elk decaying in the stream. Here there had been a cessation of natural balance and living harmony; no order of growth remained, for without a backward glance the forming soul had fled like wild creatures fleeing when the high flame roared and rolled through the tree tops.

———————

THE ALIEN

Burnt tree trunks and fireweed, near Moose Meadow, Banff National Park, AB, 1998

Two hour exposure of stars circling Polaris, Peter Lougheed Provincial Park, AB, 1998

During the August days the pines seemed never still, compelled endlessly by a gentle West wind, tip points swaying in shallow arcs against the mountain sky, persistently sighing with the mind-filling hoarseness of a water-fall.

THE ALIEN

Triple exposure with wide-angle lens on pines, Peter Lougheed Provincial Park, AB, 1998

Weathered grey, the ship-lap sides of the Powderface cabin were streaked regularly where nailheads had wept rust. Mountain spring exploded in his face. Fifteen years and he still wasn't emotionally ready for the chinook stirring over his cheek and breathing compassion through the inner self that had flinched and winced for months from the alienating stun of winter. Full reprieve! Smell, Sinclair — smell leaf mould and wet earth, singing with the menthol of spruce, bitter with the iodine edge of willow smoke from Esau's stove-pipe! . . .

It had all the surprise of young love; spring truly was like first love. . . . This wasn't really Carlyle Sinclair at all — out of his dark winter nest and into total light, eyes squinted against sun dazzle, shouldering forth and lifting upright to swing his head from side to side, testing the crystal ring of spring now with this ear, now with that one. . . .

———————

THE VANISHING POINT

Chinook arch, near Saskatoon, SK, 1981

Behind the Powderface cabin, the morning sun reflected from patches of water glinting like mirror shards scattered all the way up to the first bench. He could hear Beulah Creek now — not the usual trickle of sound, but a deeper spring surf with now and again, half-heard, the almost-human voices uncertain in stream music.

———

THE VANISHING POINT

Hand-held camera zoom on Cat Creek, AB, 1998

Camera motion on poplars, sunset light, 1981

. . . the movie advance man who had led an international covey of journalists up and down the Spray River [said]: "I don't think you Canadian people actually know or appreciate what you've got here. Terrific! You have got the sexiest scenery on this whole American continent!"

Ben stewed over that for several days . . . then came up with his story entitled "The Sex Life of Old Mount Rundle."

> *Your editor had always thought the Three Sisters were virginal, never dreamed that Edith Cavell lay in close proximity under majestic Eisenhower for sexual reasons! We have difficulty with old Flat Top and Mount Hood, about as sexual as door-knobs. We have never understood till now that the fierceness of our Chinooks was the panting of warm lust, that lodgepole and jack pine and spruce were simply arboreal erections.*

———————

ROSES ARE DIFFICULT HERE

The Three Sisters, through flower petals, Canmore, AB, 1998

Brooding sky over the Great Sand Hills, SK, 1981

Inscapes

BY COURTNEY MILNE

"Let's you and I conjure together. You watch me and I'll watch you and I will show you how to show me how to show you how to do our marvelous human tricks together."

The first and only time I set eyes on W.O. Mitchell was at one of his readings in the early 1980s in the Adam Ballroom of the Bessborough (now the Delta Bessborough) in Saskatoon. He was in his prime, put on a fabulous show, and punctuated every third sentence with a snort of snuff. He was folksy, relaxed, funny, and took great delight in playing to his audience. It was easy to love him – and his recitations became an added bonus to meeting W.O., the man. I left the hotel that evening feeling that the universe had bestowed on me a gift – permission to loosen up, to be myself, to take some risks, and to have a little more fun, especially in how I presented my craft. Little did I know then that I would be getting to know this complex person in much greater depth – through his writings, through my lenses, through his son Orm Mitchell

Self-portrait after photographing dust storm, Saskatoon, SK, 1980

(who at times is amazingly like his father), and through Barbara Mitchell, who has given me many insights on W.O. and the Mitchell family.

One phone call with Orm and Barb in August 1998 convinced me that working on *W. O. Mitchell Country* was high on my list of priorities. For the past twenty years I had spent large chunks of time recording the play of light on the fabric of the Saskatchewan prairie, but I had spent almost no time in the Alberta foothills, and had visited the Rockies more on vacation than for serious photography. Now, in keeping with my earlier inspiration more than a decade and a half before, it was time to get serious about having some fun, and to try to see the world through W.O.'s eyes.

The project heated up rather quickly. Along with my wife, Sherrill, who had done the research on several of my previous books, I met with Barb and Orm in Weyburn, in southeastern Saskatchewan. This was W.O.'s boyhood home town and the model for Crocus, the setting for his novel *Who Has Seen the Wind*. Somehow it seemed fitting that the first face-to-face encounter for the Mitchells and the Milnes, two staunch Scottish families (Milnes are descendents of the Gordons), happened to take place at McDonald's, although as far as history records, neither clan ever made hamburger out of the other! My heart was full of anticipation and my head swam in a pool of questions that I hoped Orm and Barb could answer about this enigmatic, sometimes erratic, often volatile, and always animated character called W. O. Even as we greeted each other I heard myself blurting out: "Were you ever scared of your father?" His answer came back fast! "W.O. yelled a lot when we were kids. We got used to it, but it scared the hell out of our friends!" Friends we quickly became, as I discovered in Orm the same charismatic qualities and off-the-cuff humour that had attracted me to W.O. and his books.

We were soon combing the Weyburn landscape for the places special to W.O. and particularly those that appeared in his novels. Right beside the railway bridge we found the CPR Hole which W.O. described in *How I Spent My Summer Holidays*, and we toured Uncle Jim's farm just a few kilometres south, where Brian would visit his Uncle Sean in *Who Has Seen the Wind*. I was getting excited. Exploring Weyburn, getting to know the Mitchells, and becoming familiar with W.O.'s haunts were bringing an immediacy to the project as well as a point of departure for me. I was raring to get back to the Mitchell farm to explore the interior of the old barn built by Jim Mitchell shortly after the turn of the century, with its one-of-a-kind wall constructed of concrete, the way it was done back in Ontario.

As we were saying our goodbyes from the curb in front of the old family home on Sixth Street, I asked Orm if he knew the year W.O. had left Weyburn for High River. Orm began by prefacing his answer with some early history going back to the year that W.O. and his wife, Merna, first met. As he was about to embellish the details of their courtship, Barb cut in: "I hate to sound like Merna, but this is no time for the half-hour version, Orm." We all laughed and agreed we would get the details on our next meeting.

Soon after, I returned to photograph extensively around the Weyburn area, including an outing in search of "the Indian Place" and the "Mental hole" with Isabel Eaglesham, a storehouse of local knowledge, particularly of the early days. Yet everywhere I went I seemed to bump into people who had a story about W.O. Occasionally I couldn't help becoming distracted from the photography. One memorable tale recounted how at Carlyle Lake in the Moose Mountains, one summer in his teens, W.O. and a pal sunbathed in the buff at what they thought would be a private beach. When curiosity seekers boated by, the boys got rid of their audience by jumping up, facing them, and waving enthusiastically! At that juncture, I had to remind myself I was here to photograph the land, not an illustrated history of W.O.'s youth!

Then on to Alberta where we met again with the Mitchells and explored the mountain views from High River as described in *Roses Are Difficult Here*, wandered the streams of the Highwood River valley where W.O. went fly fishing, and rose at 5:00 in the morning to catch the first light on Frank Lake, where father and son had enjoyed goose hunting together. Nowadays the lake is shared by tourists, conservationists, and members of Ducks Unlimited. As I gingerly trekked across the soft flats and crouched in the reeds at sunset, the sound of several gunshots resounded across the lake and I wondered if I was the sitting duck!

I spent several days in High River camped beside the Highwood and made trips out by bicycle with camera, tripod, and lenses in tow. On one trip I was about to set up when an overly enthusiastic dog bit me in the leg, tore my jeans, and left his mark. The owner, who had heard the commotion, seemed more concerned about defending his dog's unblemished record than about my welfare. Thinking of my jeans, you might say that

Window sill of barn at Dog Pound, northwest of Cochrane, AB, 1998

Dirt on window from dog paws, Saskatoon, SK, 1986

this book was produced by blood, sweat, and tears! We stayed in W.O.'s Calgary home and visited "Dog Pound" (without further mishap), an acreage north of Cochrane that became the setting of *For Art's Sake*. Later, with the fall colour in full swing, I explored the Kananaskis region for the first time, photographed around Banff and along Highway 1A to Johnston Canyon, then took a hop by helicopter for four days at Mount Assiniboine to catch the larch in their autumn splendour.

Everywhere I went I carried four-by-six cards with quotations chosen by Orm, Barb, and Sherrill from various W.O. novels and other publications, with his descriptions of relevant landscapes woven into the context of the stories. Each morning I would rise early to be on hand for the first light. My ritual was to pull the cards with quotations relevant to the geography for that day and to read through them several times as a way of storing pictures in my head. It brought back memories of Scott Russell and me sitting in the cloak room in grade two with a set of flash cards practising our multiplication tables. We would take turns drilling each other – the correct answer was on the back of each card. But the arithmetic of the second-grade flash cards didn't seem to be the same any more. Maybe $2+2=4$ then, but it seemed that on my new set of cards W.O.'s descriptions were providing a quality to my pursuit of landscape that made the results significantly greater than the sum of the parts.

Another challenge in this project was to overcome my fear of failure. I knew I had many strong images of the prairie landscape that I could rely on, but I had no back-ups for the foothills or the Rockies and my time flying into Assiniboine was limited, with the weather playing a crucial role. My first two days at Assiniboine had resulted in some spectacular skyscapes accented with dramatic light, but with the exception of the first ten minutes after my arrival, when I was preoccupied with getting settled in, I did not see the dazzling sunlight on the golden larch for which I had come. Because of the limited time there and the very real deadlines, my hope was quickly fading. Then something rather miraculous happened. As I began packing for the chopper flight out, the manager of the lodge appeared and said there was room for me on a flight two days later, and besides, the sun was going to shine tomorrow! I couldn't refuse.

The next morning revealed a sky that was still overcast and my heart sank. Yet as I was preparing for the day's first excursion my eye landed on one of the flash cards, one that

Spruce and larch with cliff face, Assiniboine Valley, Mt. Assiniboine Provincial Park, BC, 1998

I had not even intended to bring. I read it aloud and laughed. The quote was from Arthur Ireland, the teacher of art in *For Art's Sake*: "Do not quit. You see, the most constant state of an artist is uncertainty. You must face confusion, self questioning, dilemma. Only amateurs are confident . . . be prepared to live with fear of failure all your art life . . ." W.O. was certainly with me in spirit that day. I left the cabin immediately, tripod hoisted on my shoulder, and set out with renewed determination. Minutes later I framed an image of a mountainscape that owes its aesthetic to flat overcast light giving the trees and mountain an even tonality. Later that day the sun broke through as I climbed up to Wonder Pass and on the return trip I was able to record mountain light at its finest. Fear is an integral part of the creative pursuit and I keep learning the same lesson over and over again.

My remaining time at Assiniboine was amazingly productive. On the following morning the entire valley at Lake Magog was covered in frost, and the sun shone valiantly on mountain, lakeshore, and larch tree, illuminating the needles as the forest was transformed into shimmering diamonds.

Morning light on melting frost, near Lodge, Assiniboine Valley, Mt. Assiniboine Provincial Park, BC, 1998

Closeup of melting frost on pine needles, Assiniboine Valley, Mt. Assiniboine Provincial Park, BC, 1998

Storm over Three Sisters and Rundle Range, from Canmore, AB, 1998

Morning light on the Rundle Range from Harvie Heights, Canmore, AB, 1998

First range of Rockies, photographed near Cardston, AB, 1997

Sand dune and grasses, Spruce Woods Provincial Park, MB, 1997

Multiple exposure of autumn colours, shoreline of Bow River, Calgary, AB, 1998

Sometimes when I am out photographing I do a simple exercise in order to see things in a fresh way. I shut my eyes, swivel around with the camera to my face, then open my eyes as I peer through the viewfinder. The resulting de-composed scene can shock the senses. The focus might be off – the lines softened – perhaps the subject matter can't even be identified. No matter. What can happen is that the mix of tones, hues, and quality of light takes on a new identity, as though you are seeing it for the first time.

Impressionistic technique is not something new to me. I have been experimenting with camera movement, multiple exposures, and water reflections for most of my career. But in this book for the first time I found myself linked with a writer who invites, endorses, and applauds this way of seeing, not just with the camera but in living life creatively. I believe W.O. saw landscapes in much the same way I attempt to portray them on film. I am inspired by his textured descriptions of the land; sometimes it seems as though he has subtly layered his words on the page with a palette knife. With my photography, I am not so much interested in what objects represent, as I am in the play of light and how the subtleties of line, tone, form, and colour combine to nourish our inner landscapes. In *For Art's Sake*, W.O. writes, "He called the paintings Inscapes because they had an inner genesis, growing from him out of memory, after-images of land and sea and leaf and blade . . . 'They are intended to celebrate the human interior.' "

My several journeys to the Rockies in search of images for this book also turned my head around and woke up my senses. I ventured west unconsciously expecting to behold familiar prairie light washing over mountain topography. I found instead that mountain light has its unique identity in the interplay of mist, cloud, wind, heat, and moisture, throughout the day and as the seasons unfold. I believe W.O. fell in love with the land all over again, as I did, when he moved to High River.

One striking difference for me was that the mountain scenery receives less direct sunlight, more areas of shadow, and many more days of overcast conditions. I needed to make adjustments, both in learning to observe and in photographic technique. I paid more attention to subtlety and to attending to things at close range. A mountainside covered in spruce or pine reflects somber tones, much darker than the bright illumination of the sky. Since the latitude of colour slide film is not great enough to get an adequate exposure for both, I found myself eliminating the horizons from the frame and concentrating on foregrounds, postponing the rugged skylines for moments of special light.

Textures of larch and pine caught my eye and I found myself interpreting and express-ing them by swirling the camera, or making a number of exposures on the same frame of film. One afternoon, while working with an autumn tapestry along the Bow River in Calgary, I wondered if W.O. had seen a similar weave of colour when, in *For Art's Sake*, he has Arthur Ireland in his jail cell forming images in his mind: "At first there was just a dark curtain that persisted against his will until thousands of light dots declared them-selves, winking and blinking so that he was looking at vibrant tweed." Arthur's apparition continues with a description of clouds, very much like the ones I found at Assiniboine, never on the prairie: "In time clouds began to form and drift and fade to reappear with light that limned their outer edges, still holding darkness within themselves as they grew new shape after shape. There was colour for the first time between those two: just a hint of blue. It's gone. No. Over there. And there's faint red . . . before long he was seeing not just cloud but the long roll of surf and the snow-capped geometry of mountains."

In Arizona there is a slot canyon carved by centuries of flash floods that course through the high walls, creating gentle wave-like rhythms in the soft sandstone. The Navajo

Backlit cloud over mountain peak, from Vermilion Lakes, Banff National Park, AB, 1998

Sunset light on mountain, from Assiniboine Valley, Mt. Assiniboine Provincial Park, BC, 1998

Double exposure with camera motion on poplars, near Saskatoon, SK, 1982

Sunlight refraction on light cloud, from Lodge, Assiniboine Valley, Mt. Assiniboine Provincial Park, BC, 1998

Camera movement on fireweed, near Moose Meadow, Banff National Park, AB, 1998

name for this canyon translates as "where water paints pictures of itself." Here in the Canadian Rockies, the higher craggy mountains, like Assiniboine, paint pictures of themselves in the sky; the midday winds whip around the summit producing an everchanging gauze of mist that, infused by the backlighting of the sun, creates mountains of colour.

Those who find beauty in a landscape do so because it touches a place of beauty already within themselves. A landscape (or an image of a landscape) that appears exquisite and joyous to one viewer may seem melancholy or forlorn to another. The image serves as a mirror of the inner person. When I was photographing the fireweed on Highway 1A near Moose Meadow, just west of Banff, I became aware of a number of cars stopping at the side of the road. A dozen people filed expectantly into the woods to see what I had "found"; they seemed quite dismayed with me when I told them there was no bear, no moose, no, not even an elk, just — fireweed. Each of them was in pursuit of an experience that could mirror their inner landscapes already featuring a giant grizzly and other untamed beasts of the wild.

Afternoon light on Vermilion Lakes, Banff National Park, AB, 1998

The classic encounter happened later that afternoon as I directed my lens across the Bow Valley from a lookout above the Vermilion Lakes. As I worked feverishly to catch the strong cross-lighting before it disappeared for the day, a belligerent male voice behind me challenged: "What the hell are you doing?" I swung around to see an oversized middle-aged man in motorcycle leathers waddling towards me. I felt immediately on the defensive as I had not a single creature to display to him, but I decided, at risk of a mountainside brawl, to stand up to him. "I'm photographing beauty," I said matter-of-factly. Before he could reply a tiny woman, with tripod in hand, suddenly appeared beside us and chimed in: "Yeah, he's photographing beauty, and you know what? It's everywhere!" Totally disarmed, and unprepared for a philosophical debate, he shook his head in disbelief and disappeared on his bike, no doubt to the "real wilderness." My friendly saviour and her husband, both members of the Toronto Camera Club, were glad for the extra elbow room as the three of us joyously planted our tripods in a row, all of us basking in the light, and W.O.'s spirit hovering somewhere nearby, relishing the melodrama!

Water reflection at Vermilion Lakes, Banff National Park, AB, 1998

Water reflection at Vermilion Lakes, Banff National Park, AB, 1998

I thought I could hear him in the autumn wind that afternoon, his raspy voice quoting a line or two from *Since Daisy Creek*, just to remind us we were on the right track: ". . . call [this] the innocence of childhood. It was once natural for each of us. Now it's become unnatural, and I'm inviting you to make it natural again. Not quite the same, though. Call it the innocence of experience . . . tell the left side of your brain — the assessor, the critic — to bugger off. You are not writing [photographing] something to be shared for approval. You are simply finding. . . ."

Photographing for this book was a rare opportunity, a chance to get into the skin of some of W.O.'s characters and attempt to perceive the landscape through the eyes and from the heart of a young boy. In a nutshell, for me it was an invitation to be childlike, to try to recapture the awe of simple discoveries, the innocence that results from suspending judgement, and the challenge of expressing the experience photographically. My hope was to find images that would reflect the feeling of the prairie a half-century ago to complement the passages from *Who Has Seen the Wind*, but this pursuit proved rather difficult. Telephone poles now have a new look, with fewer crossbars, or have disappeared altogether with the advent of underground cable. Round bales have largely replaced square bales, which in turn replaced stooks many decades ago. Jet trails blaze across prairie skies, often becoming the dominant feature. Farms have been modernized, grid roads paved, the locomotive has disappeared, and even the familiar grain elevators are being abolished from the skyline at an alarming rate. But there are a few characteristics of the landscape that remain, features that allowed me to recapture the look and feel of yesteryear. The coulees and marshes look much as they always have, particularly the Souris River that W.O. visits in *How I Spent My Summer Holidays*. Weyburn has grown to become a thriving agricultural centre, but the river has the ambience of the 1930s if experienced from the water. With a bit of persistence I secured the use of a canoe for two days and drifted with a lazy current while recording the colours and textures of the water's edge. It was easy to slip into a timeless world, the contemporary life of Weyburn conveniently obscured by the proliferation of bulrushes and stately grasses on the high banks of the river.

Another way I found to induce prairie nostalgia was to explore some of the long-abandoned farmsteads that still survive the relentless onslaught of sun and wind. Spending several hours alone in a building that still harbours memories of pioneer life has indeed

Abandoned farmhouse (no longer standing) near Smuts, SK, 1979

left me with vivid memories of my own. Whether or not these derelict structures contain ghosts, they certainly feel haunted; just as I was convinced that I was truly alone, I sensed an almost inaudible whistle through the skeletal shell of the house and my heart leapt as a pigeon flapped wildly past my head. I resolved not to be deterred by the eeriness of working there. These weathered prairie hulks were so filled with the remnants of an age of hardship, I have to confess that the urge to flee was often strong, but an inner voice urged me to hold fast, reminding me that this was the heart of W.O. Mitchell country. These broken buildings, scattered around the Weyburn area and across the Great Plains, though showing the wrinkles and cracks of their age, have borne witness to the human drama, the real-life stuff of Billie Mitchell, the child, and grist for W.O. Mitchell, the author.

My time exploring the antiquated farms, the charming frontages of small towns, and the neglected corners of ranch yards, also got me pondering, "What is W.O. Mitchell country, anyway?" Perhaps it is a time as much as it is a place, an era when people were outdoors accomplishing things with their hands, where a trip to town was a big event, and there were no shopping line-ups at the general store. There was no television, so we didn't compare every facet of our lives with Hollywood, and thus we were a little more content with the few possessions and relationships we already had. Or perhaps life then was little more than real hardship, although we have this false notion that those times were better. Whichever view reflects the real history of small-town Saskatchewan, the half-baked and half-forgotten memory of those early years is, for me, W. O. Mitchell country. It is an important chunk of nostalgia, a piece of turf that lies somewhere within.

The precise geography does not really matter, nor does the time in history. Perhaps W.O. Mitchell country is anyone's and everyone's litmus years, a place where your impressions of people, events, brooding skies, grasshoppers, and new ideas are all bigger than life itself.

One of the many joys in photographing for this book was having the mandate to return to a place of simplicity within, to lie for a complete afternoon gazing at the blue beyond. My hope is that this book will portray for others the magic I felt by putting myself in Brian's shoes, and in interpreting the creation of the world according to Saint Sammy. I believe I am the richer for it and that the wealth of my experiences with the

Wide angle of abandoned house, from contemplative posture, northwest of Regina, SK, 1998

camera has given me a new sense of freedom and expanded horizons. The camera technique is not new but the commission to produce images that complement W.O. Mitchell, descriptive writer, philosopher, satirist, comedian, and hedonist, is an unqualified invitation to pursue the work closest to my heart. This book made me dig deep, have fun, and go wild. I photographed with intensity. I also revisited acres of my earlier work, some of it long forgotten. The project became a chance to reacquaint myself with an old friend, the man-of-the-prairie me that took great delight in minimalist compositions. I relived some of my sojourns in Abstractland and places of make-believe when seen through a lens. The pilgrimage to a rusted oil drum accidentally decorated with spilled paint dates back to 1979. I wonder what W.O. would have seen in the abstract white figure, or how he would have woven this enigma into the storyline of a novel. I think he would have appreciated the photograph of the brick wall. This image can be approached in several ways: enjoy the colour for colour's sake, try to decipher the words, or guess what it is. For me, this remnant of a 1940s advertisement is a throwback to the tobacco-chewing days of W.O. Mitchell country.

Brick wall and window, downtown Swift Current, SK, 1998

Spilled paint on rusted oil drum, 1979

Camera motion on wild rose bushes, autumn colours, Grandora, SK, 1997

Making this book has reminded me to continually foster that vital connection to the place I live – not just to smell the roses, but to savour the fleeting beauty of rosebushes whipped by the autumn wind. It was an opportunity to acknowledge that the natural world lives within me in the joys I experience, the magic that I touch, the awe that I recognize, the grandeur that I cannot possibly fathom – these are the elements of a soulful life. The panoramas, landscapes, abstracts, closeups, and reflections are but nature's mirrors of the internal and the eternal. The more I can fine-tune my senses and sensitize my capacity to receive, the richer and more joyous is life's journey. I believe the "litmus years" are whenever I choose to be open and vulnerable. It is the trap of getting too "busy" – not the process of aging – that prevents my litmus – and probably yours – from passing the acid test. The act of making photographs is my grand excuse to bask in the warmth and wealth of the day's first light, to refresh my soul in the gloaming, and to experience the awe. Like young Brian, I personally like to visit Saint Sammy by myself because then the time is my own – and dialogues with the universe should not be curtailed.

Multiple exposure of hoar frost on poplars, Grandora, SK, 1997

I also identify with Brian's encounters with nature, when brief moments of passion overwhelm reason. For me, it most often happens when I have framed something in the viewfinder — something strange, or inexplicable, or simply where the colours are so delicious or the textures so sensuous that my rational world can no longer contain the explosive sensations. Though it is easier for me to find pictures rather than words to put a handle on Saint Sammy's flywheel, I can at least attempt to define why I feel such an affinity for W.O., the person. You might say that he gives me permission to not have to explain. He helps me to understand that the most creative and erotic moments have no answers or definitions — they just are. Not only is the not knowing all right with him, but those experiences are to be celebrated, both for the unabashed glory of what they are, and simply because they cannot be defined.

My transformative experiences usually happen by observing not so much the object in the lens as the quality of the light. Prairie light is often rich, intense, and low-angle, particularly in winter or during a lingering sunset in June. It bathes the land with saturated

Lichen-covered rock in field, southeast of Big Beaver, SK, 1998

Frost on wild strawberry plants, near Lodge, Assiniboine Valley, Mt. Assiniboine Provincial Park, BC, 1998

Shadows of grasses on sand dunes, Spruce Woods Provincial Park, MB, 1997

colour and creates textures more real than life itself. Was it a stroll along the Souris River or was it the pure cloudless sunlight of Weyburn, Saskatchewan, that prompted W.O. to pen Brian's wonderment after the lad's visit to Saint Sammy?

"And yet for breathless moments he had been alive as he had never been before, passionate for the thing that slipped through his grasp of understanding and eluded him. If only he could throw his cap over it; if it were something a person could trap. If he could lie outstretched on the prairie while he lifted one edge of his cap and peeked under to see. That was all he wanted . . . one look. More than anything!"

The more I photographed, the more W.O. Mitchell country seemed to expand as if some benevolent spirit were annexing new territories. Yes, W.O. Mitchell country relates to a geography as big as the prairies, as grand as the foothills, and as lofty as the snow-capped peaks of the Rockies. It stretches from the all-encompassing prairie sky to the tiniest "critters." Perhaps it is also a mythical country, a candidate for the book *Legendary Places.* Its citizens are ordinary, plain-talking folk, inordinately proud of W.O., especially in what

Shadows of poplar trunks on granular snow, Beaver Creek Conservation Area, near Saskatoon, SK, 1978

Lifeless pine tree, Kananaskis, AB, 1998

Shadow of photographer on mud flats, Big Muddy Lake, near Minton, SK, 1998

223

Farm trails west of High River, AB, 1998

Gravel road near Warman, SK, 1981

you might call the capital, the "twin cities" of Weyburn and High River. W.O. Mitchell country is also the sounds and smells of the big outdoors, and the sting of the dust-thickened wind on your face. Summer gales can make your hair grow sideways (regardless of whether it is the kind that springs from your scalp or sprouts from your chin!). On one occasion I was on my stomach with a wide-angle lens, recording the topsoil lifting off a field of summerfallow. I kept shooting until the camera was so full of grit that the film would no longer advance to the next frame. When I got home I looked in the mirror — and thought I caught a glimpse of Saint Sammy about to unleash another wild and glorious tale.

Perhaps W.O. Mitchell country stretches beyond the settings of his novels and stories. An inscape, after all, pays no heed to topography, location, climate, weather, or region — it is a place within each of us, regardless of where we call home. W.O. Mitchell country is wherever little old ladies wave their arms and cry "there's beauty everywhere," or wherever a dog paints the living-room window with mud because he's overjoyed to see his master through the glass. It is wherever wind bends the willowy spines of grasses, or first frost rims the leaves of the strawberries. It is a land where winter piles up in drifts, and long blue shadows reach across virgin snows, or where a red squirrel in quest of food confronts both sub-zero chill and marauding magpies. It is wherever spring returns to the land or wherever there is even the faintest knowing that it will. W.O. Mitchell country is wherever the heat of a midday sun parches the soil and sculpts a stately pine into a silvered monument to itself, testimony to the eternal cycle of all life.

THE MAKING OF THE BOOK

Once in a blue moon elements conspire to produce something unique. This is indeed such a book – begun with a dream idea, entered into with a burst of spontaneous enthusiasm and energy, and finished off, as all good books are, with much hard work. This is a tale of an unusually close collaboration.

A few months following the death of W.O. Mitchell, Doug Gibson, who had been W.O.'s editor for many years, phoned Orm and Barbara Mitchell. What would they think, he began, about a coffee-table book called *W.O. Mitchell Country*, a book of first-class stock photographs of the prairies captioned by W.O.'s prose, with an introductory essay by them? Orm and Barbara were hesitant. It was a fascinating idea, for W.O. was a superb prose painter of his landscapes. But if this were going to be done, the book would need images that caught not only the picturesque character of the prairies, but its darker presence as well – the prairie's "awful" side felt by Brian in *Who Has Seen the Wind*. It would also have to be a book about the Alberta foothills, that other landscape that W.O. painted. Most importantly, they felt that W.O. would want a creative partner who would play with his words, who would go beyond the ordinary.

Doug wanted to adapt the idea as they suggested. A few weeks later he called to say that he had just been talking with Courtney Milne, the well-known Saskatchewan landscape photographer, who was attracted to the idea of a W.O. Mitchell country book. And, just by chance, Courtney had the next six weeks free. This felt better – a Courtney Milne book shot through the filter of W.O. Mitchell's prose. Orm and Barbara said they would think about it. Perhaps if Courtney had not called just ten minutes later and sparked an excited three-way, hour-long conversation, they would still be thinking about it! But Courtney, like W.O., is a spontaneous enthusiast. And, as W.O. would say, everyone immediately "clicked."

Quite amazingly, the book materialized, from conception to final draft, in a mere six months. Every page of W.O.'s fiction, and a great deal of his non-fiction writing, was searched for suitable quotations. Although Courtney had thousands of prairie photographs, he wanted specific ones of Weyburn, and he needed images of the Alberta foothills and mountains, new territory for him. Chaptering and thematic ordering needed to be discussed. Basic issues like the size and format of the book needed to be agreed upon. If this sounds easy — it wasn't. W.O. used to emphasize to his creative-writing students the importance of "grace" in writing, of making it all look easy, or what he called the "art which conceals art." He once had this quality brought to his attention by a seasoned harvest hand who showed him how to pitch bundles in the Dirty Thirties: "Don't git your muscles all harled up. Just grab the handle loose and easy an' let her slip through your hand easy. Do it so she looks easy but remember she shure as hell ain't."

The selection process underlined for the Mitchells the richness of the prose of *Who Has Seen the Wind*. It also verified two impressions they had about W.O.'s work from their research for the biography: that the later works, except for *How I Spent My Summer Holidays*, are less descriptive, and are dominated by narrative and dialogue; and that "The Alien," an unpublished manuscript, contains some of W.O.'s best descriptive writing — as precise and evocative about his foothills landscape as that in *Who Has Seen the Wind* about the prairies.

For Courtney it wasn't enough to shoot from abstract words. He wanted to see and feel W.O.'s actual landscapes. So two trips were planned with the Mitchells as guides to show Courtney where W.O. lived and "played" and wrote. In Weyburn, armed with Sherrill's four-by-six flash cards of W.O. quotations, the Milnes were conducted on a tour of the country that had "stained" W.O. in his first twelve "litmus years." They went to the three-storey Mitchell house, the Presbyterian church where young Billie was given a Bible for perfect attendance, and the CPR bridge from which Billie and his friends dived (stark-naked) into the Souris River hedged with cattails, then to the cemetery south of town where W.O.'s mother and father are buried, and two miles further south to Uncle Jim's farm, and out onto open prairie.

Two weeks later the Milnes met the Mitchells in Calgary and delighted them with a slide show of eight hundred Weyburn and prairie photographs. In turn the Milnes were wowed by the country around High River, the Eden Valley, and the Kananaskis. Courtney returned twice to photograph Frank Lake, the Highwood canyon, and the mountains. W.O. had introduced him to some new and stunning country.

By the end of September, eight thousand new exposures from his three photography trips were on Courtney's light board for scrutiny. He brought out ten thousand additional slides from his archives. From this combined pool of eighteen thousand slides — eighteen thousand! — he culled his favorite three thousand images.

The next slide-show editing session was in December at the Mitchell home in Peterborough where, over two days, twelve hundred photographs were analysed. Now it was time to be tough. Was the image true Mitchell territory? Did it effectively complement a particular passage from Mitchell's work? Did it fit thematically the patterns into which the book was slowly growing? Was it visually exciting? Had it appeared in another of Courtney's books? How would it fit sequentially and visually with other images? Courtney had the eye for what was photographically good, the Mitchells for what was in tune with W.O.'s sense of place.

After Peterborough about five hundred photographs were earmarked for the final edit. Before going back to the light boards at his home in Grandora, Saskatchewan, Courtney went to Toronto to meet with the key players at McClelland & Stewart. Everyone agreed with the Vice-President of Production, Krys Ross, that, on a practical note, a colour book of this size was already past the deadline for fall publication. But the excitement over the project prevailed and Kong Njo, the Art Director at McClelland & Stewart, and Doug Gibson, in his joint role as editor and publisher, agreed to come to Saskatoon and participate in the final selection and editing session in January.

The five-day marathon of editing — the last three of which involved Kong and Doug, who had fled a great Toronto snowstorm to enjoy balmy Saskatoon weather — were exhilarating and productive. And exhausting! Huge decisions were made and remade; passages were edited, reordered, and matched to photographs. Each image had to be seen in relation to the flow of the book, in terms of colour, line, and design. Two projectors beamed side-by-side images so that the vitally important double page placement could be seen.

Sherrill and Courtney juggled slides from projector to projector to try out all combinations, as everyone in the room voiced their reactions. High on the energy from this work, Courtney, recalling his early days doing research in psychology, pronounced that all our eyes were now 'tachistoscopically' trained.

Each, of course, had his little territory to protect, but there were only one or two minor skirmishes. Doug settled any ties, and final choices had to pass the approval of Kong, who quietly scrutinized the screen like a hawk hovering over a colony of prairie gophers. Perhaps the amicable tone was fostered by the comfortable surroundings provided by the Delta Bessborough. Coffee and fifteen-minute lunch breaks brought relief for tired eyes. Later, at the home of the Milnes, a little Glenfiddich went a long way towards keeping spirits buoyant as work went on at the light boards into the wee hours of the morning.

In fact, it was a great team effort — there were no high sticks and no boarding calls and Courtney certainly had the shots! His colleagues were grateful that his balance, patience, and openness to suggestions — as five other sets of eyes kicked his photographs around — were able to keep the collaborative energy working.

At the end of the session, two hundred excellent slides sat on the portable light trays — as rejects! Two hundred others, even better, had made the final cut. As packing up began, Doug stood gazing at the trays of rejects and began to laugh: "Courtney, if you had brought these rejects into M&S for a book, we would have yelled, 'Yes, yes, *yes!*'"

The introductory essays and photo captions were completed in time for the birth of the second full moon in January, rising gently, silently through a blue mist on the eastern horizon. Once in a blue moon you get a chance to play on a team like this . . .

ACKNOWLEDGEMENTS

My deepest appreciation to Agfa Inc. Canada, Manfrotto Canada, and Tamron Canada, for their ongoing support of my photography.

Many thanks to the following hotels who found "room at the inn" for this wayward photographer:

Manitoba
The Fort Garry, Winnipeg
Saskatchewan
The Delta Bessborough, Saskatoon
Perfect Inns, Weyburn
Alberta
Chateau Lake Louise, Canadian Pacific Hotels, Lake Louise
The Palliser, Canadian Pacific Hotels, Calgary
Kananaskis Lodge, Canadian Pacific Hotels, Kananaskis Country
Mount Engadine Lodge, Kananaskis Country
Heritage Inn, High River

My appreciation also goes to: Stephen B at the *Weyburn Review*; Isabel E, Edgar W , and Jack M for their memories of W.O.; the farms of Todd Lawrence, Ray Milne, Frank Yeast, and Bill Peters; Ben and Marcia at "Dogpound"; Jeff, Candis, Evan, and Kiva in Banff; Pat and Heather in Canmore; Sepp, Barbara, Lance, and Iris at Mt. Assiniboine; German, Wanda, and Holly in Calgary; Janet E, Sue K, Lorna R, Mavis N, Doug R, George T, Lori L, Natalie R, Adele C, Manfred F; and to my landscape photography students over the past twenty years, many of whom have shared my journeys to make these photographs. Thanks to Tom and Clane E for your thoroughness in researching the rare jumped-up-green plant.

On the business side, thank you to Peter G, Jim R, Aaron M, and Les W; Rob, Sam, and Murray at West Canadian Color Lab in Calgary; and in Saskatoon, to Sean and Jim at Dark Horse Studio and Randy and Laurie Ann at Chromographics.

Hooray for Orm, Barb, Sherrill, Doug, and Kong, Valerie, Krys, and the many "unseen" faces at M&S. What a team! And thanks to Mother Earth for her splendid creations — the prairies, the foothills, the mountains. . . and to the special people who added a smile, gave a hand, or simply made W.O. Mitchell country a joyous place to photograph!

Courtney Milne
Grandora, June 1999

Wood carving in W.O. Mitchell's study, Calgary, AB, 1998